Mystery Horse

Lisa Morgan

Other Books by Lisa Morgan

The Christmas Horse

Troubled Hearts

Mystery Horse

Running Wild

Trail Trouble

Please visit:

www.LisaMorganAuthor.com

Copyright © 2017 by Lisa Morgan

Published in the United States by Seaquine Publishing.

ISBN-10:0-9993988-0-6
ISBN-13:978-0-9993988-0-7

DEDICATION

To the sweet girls I meet at the horse shows. You make my day when I get to talk with you, to see you ride, and to hear your excitement when you tell me about the ribbons you won. I love to hear the stories about how your mother took your Lisa Morgan book away the night before so you'd sleep. I hope you enjoy this adventurous story. You are the reason I keep writing.

Happy reading! Love you all.
~~Lisa Morgan~~

ACKNOWLEDGMENTS

I want to thank all my readers, for you keep me dreaming about my next stories. If I ever get discouraged, I think back to your happy faces when you run up to me at horse shows and ask me when my next book will be out. This story is for you.

CHAPTER ONE

A gentle breeze blew against Kate Patrick's face as she rounded the corner of the arena. There were two more jumps left in the course, the first one a scary roll top covered in grass-like Astroturf, the second one a wide oxer made to look like a brick wall. If she managed to overcome her fear, even for a moment, she'd reach a new level in her riding.

She focused on the roll top, mentally calculating the strides so they'd hit a seamless takeoff spot. Usually Razor tossed his head to argue when she asked him to slow down, but not today. He listened. They left the ground with perfect timing, and Kate felt as if she were flying.

The second jump was easy in comparison but still big because it was wide with a dangling pole behind the painted brick box. She floated over the jump with ease. While he cantered around the corner of the arena she patted his neck with extra vibrancy. What a good boy. If he performed like that in a horse show, certainly they'd take home the championship ribbon for their division.

"Wonderful job, Kate!" Layne, her strict but outstanding trainer, yelled approval across the ring. "Go ahead and walk. You're finished."

A surge of excitement darted through Kate at Layne's rare praise. And to make the moment even sweeter, Sam was watching. He tilted back his head, let out a yelp, and clapped his hands together loudly. The instant satisfaction she experienced must be how Razor felt when she rewarded him with a firm pat on the neck. Sam made her belly swirl and her breath shorten. He was hot.

Boys were off limits, though. Her mom didn't allow her to have a boyfriend because she thought Kate was too young. For real? Kate disagreed, not that it made a difference as far as her mother was concerned. But Kate went to school with Sam, so despite her mother's rules, it was easy to see him. Plus, he rode occasionally at their barn. After a couple of months of hanging out, in Kate's eyes, they were dating.

"Great ride," Taylor, the almighty brave leader of the Horse Club, further rewarded Kate with praise. Her best friend walked her horse, Frankie, on a loose rein with her feet kicked out of the stirrups.

Kate's answer was a humble smile, but inside she was beaming. When she first received Razor as a Christmas present, not only was she too small for him, but she was afraid. What a struggle to get to this point. Building confidence enough to complete a full two-foot-six course with him was huge progress.

"Keep practicing, girls," Layne called out. The girls thanked her and Layne left the ring to head back to the barn.

They walked their horses around the arena to cool them down. Kate's heart squeezed into a tight knot when a girl named Lacey approached the ring and sat next to Sam on the bleachers. What was *she* doing here?

Lacey scooted a little too close to him, tossed her long hair back behind one shoulder, and laughed. Kate almost bit her tongue in half when Lacey touched him on his knee. The nerve. To his credit, he moved his knee away, but otherwise he didn't seem to mind her flirtatious behavior.

Trouble was brewing. Lacey was known for going after other girls' boyfriends, and didn't stop until she got the prize.

Taylor glared at Sam and Lacey, and then turned her pointed stare at Kate. The scowl challenged Kate to do something about the annoying scene unfolding in front of them. Confrontation was more Taylor's personality, a true go-getter, and Kate was naturally more laid back, caring. Well, not when it concerned her man. Kate nudged her tired horse forward and stopped directly in front of Lacey.

Lacey ignored Kate. Some people were so rude.

"Great ride," Sam said to Kate, a small smile forming on his lips to expose straight teeth. "Before long you'll bring home all the blue ribbons."

Lacey rolled her eyes, which Sam of course didn't see. "With a horse like Razor, that would be expected," Lacey said sweetly.

Kate clenched her teeth. She heard the backhanded compliment despite the rich, smooth tone Lacey delivered the insult with. She was saying that Razor was an easy ride and with his talent, all Kate had to do was hold on and she'd win. That simply wasn't true.

"Thanks," Kate said to Sam. Two people could play the ignoring game, and she wasn't going to fall into Lacey's trap. If Kate replied, no matter what words she chose, Lacey would twist them around and make Kate look stupid. No thanks.

Taylor cued her horse to move closer to Kate— a united team. That was what good friends were for. In general, Taylor was a direct, straight-forward person, and Kate was glad her friend was by her side.

"What brings you to the barn, Lacey?" Taylor asked. "I haven't seen you ride in over a week."

Yay, Taylor! And she was right. The equestrian sport took dedication. Riding one time a week was fine if you were just learning or maintaining muscles, but once you reached the level of showing, most girls rode several times a week. Sam, one of the best junior riders Kate knew, rode at least that, probably more.

"Blue's lame," Lacey offered. Blue wasn't Lacey's horse; she was a lesson horse, so if Lacey really wanted to ride she could have chosen another schooling horse.

"Seems if you want to stand a chance of competing against Kate and Razor, you better start practicing." Taylor was ruthless.

"Well, that was rude." Lacey got up and stepped down from the bleachers. At least she moved away from Sam. Taylor was the best.

Sam looked confused by what just happened.

"I'll see you at school, Sam." Lacey bounced away and headed toward the barn. Wonderful, they'd see her again when they finished cooling out their horses.

Sam nodded but didn't say anything. His mom pulled up in a fancy long car and waved him over. "Well, see you tomorrow," he said to Kate.

Hopefully he'd text before that, but if not, so be it. She was not going to chase him. And if the horrible Lacey chased and won him, then he deserved her. At least that was how Kate wanted to feel about the situation. The truth? Lacey was a threat.

Kate's muscles quivered. She wasn't sure if it was from the bad vibes about Lacey, or if it was because the sun was sinking fast and there was a chill in the evening air. Either way, it was time to return to the barn before the sun disappeared behind the trees. They needed light to navigate the path back to the stable.

They rode their horses through the open arena gate and toward the barn. Kate loved living in an equestrian neighborhood with its two barns and lush turnout pastures. Sometimes, when Kate felt brave, they rode the trails that wound along the backside of the neighborhood, connecting to other trails along the way. For safety reasons, and partly because Kate was still afraid to ride on trails, she preferred the enclosed, covered arena. It was big enough for eight or so horses to canter during a horse show and not feel cramped.

Her mom always said to be thankful for what you had because people often took blessings for granted, or they focused on negative aspects of what was missing in their lives instead of gratitude.

Well, Kate was grateful to own Razor, her best friend. She slid her hand down his soft neck.

When the metal from his horseshoes clanked against the asphalt parking lot, the moment of deep, inner thought disappeared. They stopped the horses in front of the barn and dismounted. To Kate's relief, most of the boarders had gone, and Lacey was nowhere in sight. There were two barns, one out back, and because of the layout, downhill. It was a bigger barn where most of the older girls hung out. Strange how the barns naturally separated them into different age groups—the smaller barn elementary and middle school kids, the larger barn advanced middle school and high school girls. Maybe Lacey was stalking the big barn, making friends with older girls, not that Kate cared.

They led their horses into the small barn and cross-tied them in the aisle near their stalls. Candice Parker, who was also a member of the Horse Club, was there brushing Spirit. Candice leased the pony from Kate after she'd outgrown him and received Razor for Christmas. At first, Kate had to admit, she was jealous of Spirit's obvious affection for the other girl, but after getting to know Candice better, Kate understood why the pony liked her so much. She was a sweet kid. She was a couple of years younger than Kate and Taylor, but at least she was mature.

After a while the few remaining people cleared out of the barn. It was Sunday evening after all, a school night. It had already grown dark outside and Kate pulled on a pullover to ward off the chill in the air. From nowhere, a boom of thunder clapped overhead, startling Kate. Where had that come from? Rain began pounding on the tin roof of the barn, making it difficult to have a conversation over the loud noise. A floodlight outside the barn lit up a small portion of the parking lot, highlighting a sheet of rain pouring down.

"I'm glad we're inside," Kate said, speaking loudly, as she put the finishing touches on Razor's coat with a soft brush.

"No kidding," Taylor yelled back. "That was close." She unhooked the crossties, letting them fall free so they clanked against the wall, and returned Frankie to the stall. She pulled off the halter and closed the stall door behind her. Frankie went to the door and peered out the bars, her ears perked forward as she stared out the barn door. What was she looking at?

Another clap of thunder cracked overhead.

From outside, a whinny rang through the dark night. The sound of hooves thundering across asphalt parking lot echoed with urgency.

"There's a horse in the parking lot!" Taylor yelled.

Before Kate left Razor's side to investigate, a mud-colored horse galloped through the barn door. He stopped dead in his tracks when he saw them, his wet feet hitting the concrete aisle and causing him to slide.

He froze, shaking, with his front legs sprawled outward. A snort rang through the chilled air, a trail of breath funneling from his nostrils. The barn light danced across his backside and brushed the tips of his mane. He looked wild, mysterious.

Where had he come from? Someone was missing an attractive horse and was sure to be looking for him. But who?

CHAPTER TWO

"Whoa, buddy." Taylor held out her hand to try to calm the horse.

The whites of his eyes were showing. He was terrified and needed to calm down before the girls were safe to approach him.

He snorted again, his head held high with his neck rigid; he was ready to flee at any point.

The thunder moved off in the distance and the rain eased. The barn was eerily quiet, except for the horses in the aisle moving about, and the frightened horse standing in the doorway.

"Everything's okay, boy." Taylor spoke in a calm, reassuring voice and the horse lowered his head some. "That's right. Relax. No one here is going to hurt you." Taylor kept her hand stretched out low and took a slow step toward him. He didn't react so she stepped forward again.

He didn't wear a halter, so there was nothing to grab hold of.

Spirit started dancing in place in the crossties. Little Candice tried to calm him but was unsuccessful. He stepped back, causing the crossties to pull against him.

"Unhook him, Candice," Kate said. The girl followed her instructions and the pony calmed somewhat. They needed to keep the mystery horse from spooking the other horses. If they could only catch him, that would help.

Leaving Razor in the crossties, Kate walked to a nearby stall of a horse who was about the same size as the gorgeous one standing in the aisle. To avoid spooking the mystery horse and making him bolt, she gently removed a halter off the hook. Slow, measured movements were best. Despite her attempt to remain calm, her heart pounded inside her chest. It wasn't every day a horse galloped into their barn!

She resisted the urge to approach the horse with the halter, resisted the temptation to grab hold of him by wrapping the rope around his neck. She stood still until his head lowered more.

"Good boy," Kate said. She was feeling braver than usual. There was something about the horse that gave her a sense of safety. Kate reached out and touched the side of his face with her hand. She rubbed him lightly at first, and when he leaned into her touch, she scrubbed his face harder and giggled. He was a ham, for sure.

"Kate," Taylor warned when he lifted his head slightly. "Let him come to you."

Kate followed Taylor's suggestion. She planted her feet in place and held the halter low. The horse tossed his head, his eyes growing wide for a moment, but he calmed quickly from Kate's soothing voice and her hands rubbing his face.

"You're okay," she said. "I'm not going to hurt you." Kate continued to love on his face with her hands, and when he lowered his head again, he allowed her to rub his forehead. He loved it so much, in fact, that he started rubbing against her as if she were a scratching post. She chuckled lightly and slipped the nose piece of the halter over his muzzle. He didn't seem to mind, so she continued until he was fitted with the halter. It was obvious he belonged to someone who at least haltered him often.

She gave a little tug on his lead rope to ask him to lower his head even more, wanting full relaxation.

Kate glanced over his body to see what kind of shape he was in. He was skinny, his flanks sucked in with his ribs showing. She let her gaze run down his legs to his overgrown feet. His shoes were loose and the nails were working their way out of the hooves. He was in serious need of a farrier.

"What are we going to do with him?" Taylor asked.

Candice hooked Spirit back up to the crossties and began grooming the pony again. She didn't speak but absorbed everything going on around her. The pony relaxed more now that the mystery horse wasn't loose and the storm moved off in the far distance.

"I don't think Layne is here," Taylor said. She approached the mystery horse and touched him on his neck. When he met her touch with anticipation, she began to give him a good rubdown. He leaned into her more, loving the attention.

"Layne left right after our lesson," Kate said, admiring the mystery horse's sweet personality. "No adult appears to be around, at least not in the small barn." The mystery horse was enjoying his rubdown so much that Kate handed Taylor the lead rope. "I'll look in the large barn to see who is here." At Taylor's nod, Kate stepped away. Before she left the barn, she studied her own horse. Razor's head was up, with his ears perked toward the new horse.

"Candice, will you watch Razor while I'm gone?" Kate asked.

"Of course," the younger girl said.

"Make sure he stays calm. If he gets worked up in the slightest, can you handle putting him in the stall?"

"I'll be fine," Candice said.

Candice was smaller and her safety concerned Kate. To her surprise, she was becoming protective over her newest friend. "Never mind," Kate said. She didn't want Candice to feel as though Kate didn't trust her, but she also didn't want to put the girl in harm's way, either. "He's cooled out. I was almost finished brushing him, so I'll go ahead and put him away." Before Candice responded, Kate unhooked the crossties. She returned Razor to his clean stall, the smell of fresh shavings and hay greeting them. But he wasn't interested in munching on the hay piled in the corner feeder. Instead, he stood at the stall door and watched the mystery horse as Kate slid the heavy door closed.

"Don't tell anyone about the horse, just see if there is an adult around," Taylor instructed. "I don't want a bunch of people up here. He needs to stay calm."

"Got it." Kate resisted the urge to run through the aisle and down the hill to the other barn. She attempted to calm her excitement by inhaling a long breath but the trick didn't work. She strolled past the mystery horse, who was standing quietly being rubbed, with Kate taking care not to walk too close to him in case he kicked out. They didn't know his history or what his faults were, so safety came first. That brought up the thought of wondering about his past.

Creative thoughts danced in her mind as she explored a few different reasons why the horse showed up at their barn. The most frightening thought stuck with her. What if he saw someone scary, maybe a thief, take over the farm where he lived? Perhaps someone was trying to steal him and he escaped barely. Maybe he was worth thousands of dollars, maybe an ex-racehorse, and someone wanted him bad enough to steal. Kate shook her head at the crazy story she'd created.

On a more logical note, it was most likely the storm had spooked him. He'd taken off and showed up at their barn. She was clueless as to how to find his real owners.

Kate scurried through the light rain, down the slippery hill, and into the larger barn. The aroma of hay was overwhelming, but the barn was neat and tidy as always. In comparison to the smaller barn, not only did it hold more horses, the stalls were bigger. There were actual grooming stalls so horses weren't blocking the aisle. They had two tack rooms, one for boarders and one for lesson horses, and each had tall wooden lockers to store away tack and grooming supplies.

There were a few older girls milling about but she didn't see any sign of an adult. Someone had to be there.

One of the high school girls walked out of the boarders' tack room.

"Hi, Kate," the girl said, studying Kate as if wondering why she was in the bigger barn, and so late in the evening. Kate knew everyone, even though she mostly kept to the other barn. The girl's name was Ruth, and she owned a young, four-year old dapple grey thoroughbred who was the calmest baby Kate had ever seen, not to mention talented and beautiful.

Kate acknowledged her with a nod. "Is Layne around, or is she gone for the evening?" Kate tried to appear as though she were just asking for no reason other than curiosity.

Ruth shrugged. "I think she left a while ago. Why?"

Why? Kate didn't have an answer.

She chose to ask a different question. "Are there any adults here? I need someone."

That stirred up a questioning look from Ruth. Her eyes were wide with curiosity as if Kate needed to explain.

Kate ignored the pressure to answer the question. She decided it best to remain quiet and to let Ruth fill in the silence. To make the situation worse, the dreaded boyfriend-stealer, Lacey, walked out the tack room. From the interested expression on her face, she'd overheard the conversation.

"What's up?" Lacey asked Kate.

The last person Kate wanted to talk to was the girl standing before her.

"Nothing," Kate said, trying to sound in control of the situation. "I'm trying to figure out who's here. That's all."

"Just us. Everyone else has gone home for the night," Lacey explained. "Can we help with something?"

Taylor had told her not to mention the mystery horse, so Kate shook her head. "Thanks, anyway." She twirled around on the heels of her paddock boots and started walking toward the barn door. "Have a good night." She turned around to wave goodbye and almost ran into Lacey, who was directly behind her. Couldn't she mind her own business?

Kate stopped in her tracks because it was obvious Lacey planned to follow her to the smaller barn. She decided to be direct with her. "Thanks, but I have things under control." In other words, Kate wanted her to remain there.

Lacey kept walking. "I need to go to the top parking lot, anyway. That's where I'm meeting my mom."

Taylor was going to blame Kate for encouraging Laccy to walk up there. Once she found out about the mystery horse, everyone in both barns would know, along with everyone at school tomorrow. Lacey passed her, walking with a mission. What a nosey girl.

Kate jogged uphill to catch Lacey. The plan had gone wrong. She was supposed to find a parent, lead them quietly to the top barn, and present the mystery horse. Lacey was hardly an adult.

Lisa Morgan

The outdoor light illuminated a path to the barn entrance. The girls walked through the wide door together, which made the situation worse. Candice and Taylor looked up to see who Kate had brought, Taylor's face scrunching into a tight knot but then immediately relaxing to hide her surprise. Kate shrugged from behind Lacey, trying to let Taylor know she hadn't said a word.

"Oh! What horse is that?" Lacey asked, walking straight to the mystery horse. He didn't spook; he actually seemed to welcome Lacey's attention.

"Stay back," Taylor commanded. When she used that tone no one challenged her.

Apparently Lacey was clueless to the warning in Taylor's voice. "Who do we have here?" she asked the horse directly, petting his face and neck. "Aren't you a beauty."

Kate ran her hand over her eyes to block out the scene unfolding in front of her. She was fast developing a headache.

As if things couldn't get worse, Kate's mom chose that moment to enter the barn. It was her turn to pick up the girls tonight and she was usually early. Without hesitation, she strode up to the horse.

"Yes, who is this handsome fellow?" Mrs. Patrick asked. Undoubtedly, she'd want details. Details meant trouble.

Lacey watched the girls closely to hear

firsthand the barn gossip.

"Mom, can we talk about this later?" Kate asked. Under no circumstances did she want to discuss the mystery horse in front of Lacey. In the meantime, until they could discuss in private a plan to find his owner, he could spend the night in one of the few open stalls left. Then a thought popped into Kate's mind. Didn't the horse rescue programs put questionable horses in quarantine usually? Did they need to put him in an empty stall far away from the other horses to isolate him and to protect the others?

"We need to call Layne," Taylor said. "She'll know what to do."

"With what?" Mrs. Patrick asked, her eyebrows raised. She studied the horse in question as if realizing she'd never seen him before.

Still trying to hide the truth from Lacey for the time being, Kate called her mother aside and into Razor's stall for privacy. Razor watched them from the corner, curious as to why they were in his stall with him.

In a lowered voice, Kate said, "Mom, we were brushing our horses when we heard a loud whinny and thundering hooves. The horse showed up out of nowhere. I went to the lower barn to try to find an adult, but that's when you came. We weren't sure what to do." The words spilled out of Kate's mouth in one long sentence.

Kate's mom was a horse person, having ridden

much of her life. As the story went, per her mom, once motherhood had taken over she didn't have much of a chance to ride anymore. Whenever her mother told the story to other horse mothers, it made Kate sad. Not only did the guilt gnaw at Kate, but knowing her mom stopped riding after a lifetime because of her was too much responsibility.

Kate shut out the deep sense of guilt to study her mom's serious face. That usually meant she was thinking. If anyone would understand the girls' need to help the mystery horse, it would be her own mother.

"Well, I agree with Taylor's suggestion," Kate said.

"Which is what?" her mother asked.

"To call Layne." Kate rubbed her chin while she thought of a way to ask Layne about her plan to isolate the horse in a stall. "We have no idea who owns the horse, or where it lives, so we might have to set up a safe environment to board him overnight."

She didn't dare add that they might have to take care of the horse for longer. Who knew who his owner was? How far had he travelled?

"I'll take care of it," her mother said. To Kate's relief, her mom walked out to the parking lot to make the call to Layne. Kate wasn't ready for Lacey to find out the details, although she was suspicious and probably figured out how the horse arrived.

Taylor stood there, holding his lead rope, while Lacey continued to make all over the horse, who seemed to love the attention. A softer side of Lacey was rather nice to see. Kate never knew it existed but she appreciated realizing the girl was somewhat human instead of the bully Kate thought she was.

Kate's mom came back in, shoving the cell phone into her jean's pocket. "Layne said to put him in stall number eight in the big barn."

The big barn? They had empty stalls in the small barn, and Kate wanted to keep a close eye on him. Why the other barn?

As if her mom read her mind, she said, "There are more stalls open down there to isolate him. You never know what he's been exposed to."

Kate disliked the idea of having him in the lower barn where Lacey hung out, but the choice wasn't hers to make. She petted the large, brown horse on the nose. He nuzzled her, and then buried his head in her chest. He was a sweet one, for sure. Lacey had practically glued herself to his side.

"Can I lead him?" Lacey asked.

Without hesitation Taylor handed over the lead rope, and Lacey cued him to follow her. The horse obeyed Lacey immediately. He seemed so well trained that someone had to own him.

Kate had no idea how to find his owner. She wondered how long Layne would board him. If it took more time than expected, or if they didn't find his home, what would happen to the mystery horse?

CHAPTER THREE

Kate barely contained her excitement all day at school. As soon as Taylor's mom pulled into the parking lot of the barn, and the moment the car stopped, the girls flung open the doors and hopped out. They made a mad dash past the small barn, down the hill, and into the big barn. They knew better than to run through the barn, but they walked as fast as possible.

They came to an abrupt stop in front of the new horse's stall. The gorgeous animal greeted them at the door. Kate stuck her fingers between the bars to pet his nose. To her surprise, he stuck his tongue out to lick Kate's hand. She giggled. He was definitely Mr. Personality. Difficult as it would be, she needed to guard her heart where he was concerned. She was already falling head over heals in love with him.

"We need a name for him," Kate said. She grabbed hold of his tongue and held it. He didn't seem to mind, wiggling his lips to mouth her hand.

Kate laughed.

"How about Lightning?" Taylor suggested. "He came in like a storm of his own."

"Thunder!" That was a perfect name for him. "How about Thunder?" Kate asked, excited by the name. Not only had his hooves sounded like rolling thunder as he galloped across the asphalt last night, he flashed into their barn to make his presence known just as the storm had."

Taylor's eyes widened. "Perfect."

Lacey scooted out of the boarder's tack room and made her way toward them. "What's perfect?"

"We named the new horse Thunder," Kate explained. "The way he ran into the barn last night, his galloping hooves had sounded like thunder rolling in."

She was afraid of Lacey making a negative comment, rejecting the name, but to Kate's surprise, she said, "Love it. The name fits him well."

Taylor didn't answer but smiled as she grabbed the halter from the hook hanging on the stall door. "Want to get out and take a walk, Thunder?" Taylor asked, trying out his name. "Yep, the name rolls right off the tongue, just the way you rolled in here."

The horse nuzzled Taylor's hair and she laughed.

"His nickname is Mr. Personality," Kate added. "Does anyone have extra brushes that we can donate to him?"

"Yes!" Lacey said, her enthusiasm bubbling over. "I have a couple of old ones I never use. Be right back." She whirled around and disappeared into the boarder's tack room.

Kate wondered why she had brushes in the boarder's tack room when she didn't own a horse. Maybe she shared a locker with someone who did. Anyway, she was glad she had extra brushes.

Sure enough, she returned from the tack room carrying what looked like a hard brush, a soft brush, and a hoof pick.

"Do you think Layne would mind if we cross tie him on the last set in the aisle?" Lacey asked. "The stalls are empty back here, so he wouldn't be exposing another horse to anything."

"I was going to walk him around for exercise and to clear his mind from standing in the stall," Taylor said. "But if he stands quietly, I don't think Layne would mind." She led him to the crossties and clipped them to his halter. Good boy that he was, he stood still.

Kate chose a brush from the small pile that Lacey had placed on the ground near the stall. She ran the soft brush across his face, the dried dirt coming off in a cloud of dust. He closed his eyes, thoroughly enjoying the rub. "With manners like his, he's used to being brushed."

"I agree." Taylor was brushing his right side

with the hard brush, and Lacey was picking his feet. He looked as though he were at a carwash, getting the full treatment.

"What are we going to do about finding his owner?" Lacey asked, her eyebrows drawn together in concentration at the difficult job of removing caked dirt from his hooves.

Kate chewed on her lower lip while her creative mind worked overtime. "We could hang fliers with a picture of him in the feed store and on bulletin boards at local stables."

Taylor nodded. "Knowing Layne, I bet she's asked local trainers already, spreading the word." Taylor moved to the other side of Thunder and began brushing off dried mud from his coat. A little cloud of dust hovered around him.

His fur had matted clumps underneath. He'd benefit from a soapy bath, maybe even a full-body clip. Kate would bet he'd look like a different horse shaved. Not that he wasn't beautiful, because he was, but someone had neglected him lately.

"His feet are a mess," Lacey said, placing his back foot on the ground after she'd finished picking it. "His front shoes are loose and about to come off. He's barefoot in the back and in need of a good trimming."

"I wonder how long he's been roaming around loose," Kate said. He was a couple hundred pounds underweight. She'd noticed this morning he had picked his hay clean from the rack and from the surrounding area underneath where most horses left untouched random pieces of fallen hay in the shavings.

Taylor shrugged. "I don't know but his care has been ignored."

Layne entered the barn and joined the girls. "I've put the word out, but so far no one knows this horse." Layne didn't touch him but her eyes roamed over his body, undoubtedly taking in his condition. "Do not get attached to him," she warned. He'll be leaving one way or the other."

What did she mean?

"Where will he go?" Taylor asked, her voice shaky. "If you don't find his owner, where will you send him?"

"To a horse rescue. I have a friend who takes in neglected animals." Layne picked up his feet and studied them. "I'll have the farrier look at his feet in the morning. The least we can do for this big guy is to put new shoes on him."

"Why a horse rescue?" Kate asked, sighing in disbelief. "Why can't he stay here? We'll take good care of him." She realized she spoke for the other girls but she was sure they felt the same way. That was an important role in being a member of the Horse Club—they helped out the community when needed.

"That's noble but he can't stay here for free."

Layne was always business minded.

There was no way the Horse Club could pay to board a stray horse. Board was expensive. Often she overheard her parents complaining about the cost of Razor's bills. Even if they did chores around the barn, there was no way to afford board, not to mention other expenses such as farrier bills for horse shoes, and vet bills for immunizations twice a year.

"I'll keep asking around, but if I don't hear something about his owner in the next couple of days, he'll have to go to the horse rescue." Layne shoved her hands in her jean pockets, as if trying not to touch the horse on purpose to avoid emotional attachment.

"His name is Thunder," Kate said. Maybe if she personalized him, Layne would allow them more time. "We're going to put up fliers at the feed store and at the local barns." Layne needed to know they were trying to find his home.

Layne frowned. "The fliers are a good idea, but like I said, don't get attached to him. I know that's hard, and it's exciting to have a mystery horse show up at the barn, but he can't stay."

It was Kate's turn to frown. Layne was so difficult sometimes. Didn't she have a heart? Kate wanted to ask how she could send the horse off to a rescue, but didn't dare. One thing was for sure, Kate wasn't about to let that happen. She didn't know how to stop it, but she'd find a way.

"Why don't you saddle up and ride your own horses?" Layne asked. Obviously her plan was to distract them from Thunder. "They need to be ridden," she added to convince them. In other words, stop focusing so much on a horse that would leave soon and pay attention to their horses.

"I don't have a horse to ride," Lacey stated. "Blue is lame."

Layne stared at her as if to warn against even thinking about mounting Thunder. "If you want to ride Willie, you can. The rest of you have horses that need attention."

Kate knew that Lacey despised riding Willie. She was a medium-sized pony that was old and barely moved. She required an excessive amount of encouragement, along with using a riding crop and spurs when needed.

As if Layne read Kate's mind, she added, "Riding Willie will be good for your legs, Lacey. She'll make them strong." At that, Layne whirled around, dismissing them as she power walked out of the barn.

Lacey and Taylor continued brushing Thunder in silence. When they finished, Taylor suggested they take him for the walk she'd promised him.

"What about Layne?" Kate asked. She was the rule follower of the group. Taylor, by nature, was the one who liked to break them. "Layne said we need to ride our own horses." Kate spoke louder as if to prove a point.

Taylor huffed under her breath. "It was a suggestion. That's all. She didn't say we couldn't walk or groom him. She wants to make sure we ride our own horses, and we will." Taylor unhooked the crossties. "My mom isn't coming for a couple of hours, so that's plenty of time."

"Me too," Lacey agreed. "I'd rather ride this guy, but who knows if he's ever been mounted." Thunder nudged Lacey's shoulder as if to say, "Are you joking?"

"Well, are you coming, Kate?" Taylor asked, heading toward the barn door with Thunder.

Kate was uncomfortable going against their trainer's wishes, but Taylor was right. Layne didn't say they couldn't continue to take care of him. She recommended they not get attached to him. That was easier said than done, of course, but at least the girls weren't breaking the rules.

Kate didn't answer but followed behind, keeping enough distance in case Thunder decided to kick. Again, they didn't know him, or his faults.

Taylor led him out back to a narrow patch of grass to let him graze. He chewed fast and hard, as if he hadn't eaten in a week. Perhaps he hadn't. Maybe he had been loose for a while. Perhaps he came from an abusive, neglectful home. The truth would eventually surface, for that Kate was sure.

CHAPTER FOUR

A couple of days later, Layne delivered bad news to the girls. "I'm sending the mystery horse to my friend's house, the one who rescues horses."

"No!" all three girls yelled at once. They were standing in front of Thunder's stall. He watched through the bars on his door with his ears perked as if he understood what Layne said.

Layne stared at them for a long moment. "I told you he was leaving. Not to get attached."

Kate wondered again how Layne allowed herself to be so coldhearted. Maybe that was too harsh but right now that word fit her perfectly. Kate supposed Layne was doing her job, which was, after all, running a barn. Kate understood their trainer's decision to a point, but the emotional part of knowing Thunder was leaving was difficult to handle. Kate fell in love with horses easily, which is why she leased Spirit to Candice. Plain and simple,

Kate wasn't able to sell her pony once she'd outgrown him.

Thunder snorted through the bars of his stall door. He made sure to share his opinion in the discussion.

"He's telling us he wants to stay here," Kate said, sticking her finger through an opening between the steel bars and rubbing his nose. He wrapped his tongue around her finger, making Kate giggle.

Layne crossed her arms. "Kate," she warned. "He leaves this weekend. He'll do well at my friend's house. Promise."

Kate fought the urge to tell her that he'd be better off here, where the Horse Club girls could watch over him. He was already starting to gain a little weight and acting friskier—a sign he was feeling healthier. Earlier today, when they'd grazed him on the hilly patch of grass again, he wasn't chewing as fast and, unlike before, he allowed them to pull his lead rope to steer him away. He was also hopping around, full of energy, when Taylor led him to graze. With progress like that, Kate preferred to see him stay.

"What about the headway he's made?" Kate challenged.

Layne narrowed her eyes. "My friend handles rescues all the time. She's used to putting on weight and working with them. If his owner doesn't come forward, she will find him a good home."

"He has a good home," Lacey said, siding with Kate.

Layne let out a long breath of air as if giving up trying to convince them. "Focus on riding your own horses." With that, she left the barn.

"We need to come up with a plan," Taylor said.

Kate didn't like the tone in her friend's voice. Sometimes Taylor had daring ideas that got them into trouble. Kate was almost afraid to ask. Against her better judgment she braced herself for the answer. "What do you have in mind?"

"Not sure yet," Taylor said, but the slant of her eyes made Kate concerned.

The three girls remained silent, each one forming a plan to keep Thunder at their barn.

"I don't think Layne will change her mind," Lacey said, sitting down on the edge of the tack trunk in front of Thunder's stall. She swung her leg back and forth with rapid force.

"I agree," Taylor said with the slant in her eyes still visible. She leaned her back against Thunder's stall door with her hands buried deep into her jean's pockets. One foot rested on the other, wiggling back and forth.

Kate knew that look well. When her friend started wiggling her foot, she was planning something dangerous.

"We've heard no response from the signs your

mom hung up," Lacey said to Kate. Kate's mother had agreed to deliver them to the local feed store and barns while the girls were in school. "It's almost as though Thunder came from nowhere. I mean, he belongs to someone. But who?"

"Maybe his owner doesn't want him anymore," Kate offered. She stood between Taylor, who still leaned against the stall door, and Lacey, who sat on the tack trunk, her leg still in motion while she thought. Kate stuck her finger through the bars of the stall to play with Thunder's lip again. That seemed to be his favorite game. He nipped it playfully. Kate watched him closely to make sure he didn't take a bite out of her, but he seemed to be enjoying the attention without trying to harm her.

"We need to bypass Layne," Taylor said, leaning against the stall door.

Bypass Layne? What in the world was Taylor thinking? No matter what, if they dodged their trainer, the crazy plan would be sure to backfire. Kate wasn't interested in bypassing anyone, but at the same time she was curious about the crazy plan her best friend had likely come up with. "What do you mean?" Kate asked, knowing full well that once she heard the answer there'd be no turning back. When Taylor voiced an idea, she usually followed through.

Taylor stopped wiggling her foot, a dead giveaway that the plan was already set in motion in her mind. "Well…" Taylor hesitated. Obviously it was a foolish idea if she paused before saying it out loud. "There's an abandoned barn on the backside of old man Brown's property."

Kate strained her mind to remember the barn. They've explored the entire neighborhood, even the short trails that dead ended into people's backyards. What was she talking about?

"Remember the old dirt road that used to be a wagon trail? It runs along old man Brown's property, up the hill, and around the side of his house," Taylor said, now standing upright and looking as though she were struggling to contain her excitement. "At the bottom, by the larger horse pasture, there is an overgrown grass road that leads off into the woods. Remember?"

It had been a long time ago since they'd ridden on that old road, Kate had completely forgotten about the barn. "Yes," she answered with caution in her voice. Where was her friend going with this idea?

"I remember that barn!" Lacey added. "It's hidden from his house by the woods but sits in a clearing."

Taylor's foot started wiggling again even though she was standing upright. That took talent. "Yes. It would be a perfect place to hide him."

Kate gasped. Taylor wanted to hide Thunder? She had to be joking!

"We could take turns feeding him before and after school," Taylor continued. She ignored Kate's reaction and kept talking. "The barn is a mess and we'd have to clean it up."

The last time Kate had seen the barn, probably over two years ago, it was solid but covered in vines. There were a couple of stalls and a small storage space where someone had probably stored feed and possibly their saddles at one time. The room had a door that locked to keep horses from attempting to steal food if they escaped their stalls at night. The stalls were interesting. They had stall doors opening to a barn aisle, but the cool thing was that each stall had individual back doors, which split into two halves, the top half opening separately into a window. The doors could be tied open, allowing access to small, individual enclosed runs, or kept closed to keep the horses warm in the winter.

The barn, after a lot of work to clean it up, would be perfect to hide Thunder, not that Kate was even considering such an insane idea. Not only would it be hard to feed him in the mornings before school, Thunder would be alone. Horses were herd animals and enjoyed being with other horses. And a bigger concern was how much trouble they'd be in when someone found out they were hiding him in someone else's barn. And someone would find out.

"No way," Kate said. "We'd be grounded for

the rest of our life."

Lacey continued to sit on the edge of the tack truck, rocking her leg back and forth. She must have adopted Taylor's habit of moving her foot when she was thinking. Lacey breathed slowly to stay calm, not saying a word. Was she considering the crazy idea, or trying to figure out a way to back out gracefully?

Taylor ignored Kate and stared at Lacey, waiting for a response. When no response followed, Taylor finally asked, "What are your thoughts?"

Lacey looked up, a frown on her face and her eyes narrowed. "It sounds risky. Kate's right; our parents will ground us for a long time if they find out."

Not one to take rejection easily, Taylor crossed her arms. "Then you're okay with Thunder being sent to a rescue?"

"I didn't say that." Lacey scooted off the tack trunk, taking a moment to brush the dust off the backside of her riding pants, and then began pacing the aisle. "I mean what choice do we have?" she asked Taylor. "Our trainer suggests he go to a rescue. The decision is hers."

Taylor huffed, her arms crossed so tight across her chest that Kate wondered if it caused her physical pain.

"I can't believe you both," Taylor said, arms still wrapped into each other. "He's a nice horse, well behaved, and he found *us*. He didn't find the rescue."

"So you think it's meant to be that he showed up here?" Kate asked. She believed in faith, so there might be truth in what Taylor was saying.

"Exactly." Taylor angled her body toward the barn door as if convinced of her decision and ready to end the discussion. Then she glanced back and added one last comment. "Layne suggested we focus on our own horses. Instead of riding in the arena, why don't we ride on a trail ride. We can check out the old barn."

Taylor was stubborn at times, apparently set on the idea of hiding Thunder. How would they pull that off? Kate thought of numerous problems. For one thing, what excuse would they use to explain Thunder's sudden disappearance? And the mornings were already busy. How would they get away before school to feed him? It was hard to imagine how they'd have time to clean his stall, groom and feed him after school, along with riding their own horses and finishing homework. The plan was nuts, not to mention overwhelming. And dishonest.

Kate brought up her questions even though Taylor started heading toward the barn door.

"Let's have a Horse Club meeting tonight at my house," Taylor suggested. "How about after dinner?"

"What about Candice?" Kate asked. "She's a member of the Horse Club, so she needs to be included in a meeting. And Lacey isn't a member, so technically she isn't supposed to attend."

Taylor stopped and turned back to look at Kate. "Let's just call it a get together then. Candice is too young. It's a risk that she might slip and tell her mother. Also, I think it's important for Lacey to be included. After all, she already knows our plan and we need her help."

Lacey smiled. Kate suspected she wanted to be a member of the Horse Club, but Kate had never gotten along well with the older girl before and didn't want her to join the club. She belonged to a different group of girls who were all older and behaved rather snobbish toward Kate. If she added Sam to the situation, that complicated Kate's feelings. She was protective over her boyfriend along with experiencing a big dose of jealousy after Lacey practically threw herself at him. If Kate had to pick, there were a lot of other people besides Lacey that she'd rather hang out with.

Taylor seemed to read Kate's mind. "Right now the three of us need to keep this a secret and work together. What do you think about a trail ride over to old man Brown's barn? I really believe Thunder found us for a reason."

That was the one point Kate agreed with. Thunder found them for a reason. Against her better judgment, and because she was half in love with Thunder already, she agreed to the plan. Once they removed him from the safety of the main barn, there was no turning back.

CHAPTER FIVE

Kate was nervous about the trail ride in more ways than one. Fear was always part of the experience but now Lacey was joining them. No way did Kate want her to know about the fear issue she dealt with daily. If she could only pretend to be brave, Lacey wouldn't know the truth.

The girls finished tacking up their horses, Kate taking longer than usual to delay the ride. Little Candice asked to join them but Taylor had to encourage her to ride with someone else. It was best if the girl enjoyed riding without worrying about hiding a horse from adults. Secrets were a bad idea.

Kate led Razor out of the barn and into the parking lot where Taylor waited. At least she wasn't the last one to mount today; Lacey was still in the barn. Kate pushed her fear aside and climbed onto her horse, who stood like a perfect gentleman, just waiting. What a good boy. When she'd first bought him he used to walk off with impatience.

Lacey left the barn and mounted her horse. Before long they headed down the narrow trail at the end of the parking lot. It wound its way through the trees, crossed over a small creek with a horse-friendly, grassy bridge, and deeper into the woods. The trail snaked behind several fancy houses and spilled out onto the old wagon trail that used to lead to a homestead, which no longer stood.

A real estate developer had built the entire neighborhood on a large piece of farm land that dated back to the civil war. One part of the land, now next to a vacant lot with new houses nearby, had a half-hidden, old cemetery set off in the nearby woods. Every time the girls rode past, Kate thought it was creepy but fascinating.

They followed the wagon trail to old man Brown's property. The house was three stories with rounded towers on the four sides of the house, resembling a modern-day castle. There were big windows in the towers overlooking the man's horse pastures. They'd have to be careful sneaking Thunder to the old barn because if the man glanced out his window, he'd be able to see them pass by his lower pasture. The barn was well hidden on the overgrown trail, and as long as Thunder was somewhat quiet, the man would never hear the horse.

They rode past the lower, biggest horse pasture.

There were three horses grazing happily until one of them spotted the girls. All three horses glanced up, ears pointed at them, watching. Kate hoped the horses didn't call out to each other, and to her relief, they stayed silent as they studied the intruders. At least Thunder would have horses nearby that he could smell and possibly hear, so he wouldn't be alone completely.

Taylor led the way and turned down the straggly, overgrown path. It wasn't a long one but a tangle of trees, debris, and bushes discouraged the casual trail rider from wanting to explore farther. They made their way down the path and the old barn came into view. Kate slowed Razor to study it. She imagined Thunder sticking his nose out of the nearest window to greet them each day. Were they really going to follow through with this insane plan?

Taylor climbed off Frankie and tied her to a tree with a halter she had brought along. They always carried halters in case they wanted to stop, and packed food and water if they were on a longer ride. They learned to prepare well because more than once they'd gotten lost and hadn't had water or anything to eat. They'd never make that mistake again.

Kate climbed off, followed by Lacey. Lacey had never ridden with them before and was about to get a quick education on the adventures of the Horse Club, not that Lacey was a member. Kate was proud that she'd hidden her fear of trail rides successfully. Of course the fear had surfaced here and there, it always did, but what an accomplishment. Even Razor seemed to notice the difference in her confidence. Maybe riding with an older girl forced Kate to be brave.

"This place is in worse shape than I thought," Taylor said. "It's been a while since I've seen it."

Kate analyzed the barn while holding Razor, noticing all the bushes growing against the side. The structure still appeared strong, but it was definitely neglected. "I don't think we'd need to remove all the growth from the sides of the building," Kate said. "If we make sure the window is clear so he can safely stick his head out, that should work." She slipped the halter on Razor and tied him a tree somewhat close to where Frankie was tied. Lacey followed her lead and tied her horse up too.

"It's beautiful." Taylor stood still, staring at the building with a smile on her face. "We can make sure to clear the vines from the entrance. Who knows what the inside looks like, though."

The three of them approached the barn, Taylor leading the group. The doorway wasn't too tangled, but a small, fallen tree covered a portion of the entrance. The three of them should be able to drag it into the woods.

They climbed over the tree and entered the

barn. The lighting was dim, making it difficult to see well until their eyes adjusted to the low light. "We'll have to clean his stall and take care of him before dusk," Kate suggested. "Otherwise we won't be able to see well enough. I'm sure there isn't electricity here."

"Even if there was electricity, we wouldn't want to use it," Lacey said. She'd been quiet most of the ride. "Someone might notice an unfamiliar light coming from this direction."

"True," Taylor said. "We don't want to attract anyone's attention."

"Yeah, that would defeat the purpose of hiding Thunder," Kate added. She glanced around the inside of the barn and sneezed. "This place is going to take some work."

"I wish I'd thought to bring a flashlight," Taylor said. "We'll have to remember that." She opened an old tack room where the farmer likely stored feed and supplies at one time. The door was intact and seemed to be in decent shape.

The room brought up another concern. "What are we going to do about feed?" Kate asked.

Taylor shrugged her shoulders. "Any suggestions?"

Lacey spoke up. "I have a friend who can drive. I bet I can convince her to make a trip to the feed store for us. I'll have to think of a way to ask that doesn't make her curious." Lacey picked up an old shovel and studied it for a moment before she placed it back against the wall. "How are we going to pay for food and shavings?"

"I have ten bucks," Taylor offered. Kate knew she babysat last weekend and had earned the money from the Snyder's. They had twin boys, so that was hard-earned money.

"I have eight dollars," Kate added. She had been saving part of her allowance for a show bridle for Razor. "How much do feed and shavings cost?"

"I don't know," Lacey said, "but I have ten dollars too. That should be more than enough to start out. We'll also need to buy hay."

This was getting expensive. How long did they plan to hide Thunder?

"We'll have to come up with a way to earn money," Taylor said. "That's going to be difficult because we'll be busy taking care of him and doing homework."

The thought was overwhelming.

"Not to mention riding our own horses," Kate added.

"We can do this," Lacey said. Apparently she was on board now with hiding Thunder. Whatever concern she had before seemed to disappear.

"Instead of meeting tonight at my house," Taylor said, "let's meet back here after dinner. We need to get started cleaning the barn."

"Let's bring brooms, a hammer, and nails,"

Lacey said.

"Work gloves," Taylor added.

Kate's mind spun around in circles. "How are we going to sneak those things past our parents?" She wasn't on board yet with the idea of hiding a mystery horse in someone else's barn.

Taylor swiped her hand across the topside of a dusty feed bin, and Kate sneezed. The old barn was aggravating her allergies.

"The hammer, nails, and gloves should be easy. We can hide them in a backpack," Taylor said, opening the bin and peering inside. "This is a perfect place to stash his feed so it's safe from mice."

Kate refused to be distracted by Taylor. She pushed the question a little more. "What about brooms? That's a little difficult to hide in a backpack."

Taylor snapped the lock on the bin and turned to study an old dusty saddle stashed in the corner, still on a saddle rack. "Why don't we meet at the main barn then. We can use their supplies and carry them here. It's not too far of a hike. We'll have to walk here daily anyway to feed Thunder, so we might as well get used to it."

No one seemed to notice, or maybe they didn't care, that Kate hadn't agreed to the plan yet. "I don't know about this idea," Kate said. "It's involved and overwhelming."

"I wonder why someone left an English saddle here," Taylor said, picking it up and turning it over. "It's begging to be cleaned and to be ridden in."

"Overwhelming," Kate repeated. She despised being ignored.

"Then don't do it, Kate," Taylor said, setting the saddle back in place. "If you're uncomfortable with the idea, then back out."

Back out. Kate didn't like Taylor's comment. Peer pressure loomed behind those words. Kate didn't answer. What could she say? If she *backed out*, she'd disappoint her friends, who were counting on her to help.

Taylor made her way through the dim room and to a ladder with solid wood planks that appeared sturdy. She climbed them hesitantly and peeked upstairs. "A hayloft. It's pretty cool up here," Taylor called down. She lingered on the ladder, studying the space upstairs, before backing down the steps. "We could store Thunder's hay there if we can get it up the ladder."

Lacey found a frayed broom in the corner and began sweeping. A dust cloud filled the tack room and Kate sneezed several times in a row. She had to get out of there fast before her asthma kicked in. Next time she needed to remember to bring her inhaler.

She hurried out of the tack room, glad to be away from Taylor so she could think enough to make a decision, and glad for fresh air to breathe better. The main aisle of the barn was narrow and thankfully no dust floating around, at least until they started sweeping. The stalls were solid. Each one had a square opening in the bars to dump grain into a corner feeder. Someone had cleaned the floors down to the uneven dirt and the stalls were smaller than the one Thunder was in now, but still big enough to require three or four bags of shavings to fill it deep enough for his comfort due to the hard floors. They were spoiled at their community barn. Layne had insisted on mats lining the ground, so the stalls didn't require deep shavings. Shavings cost money.

Kate wasn't going to mention the difficulties or her concerns again. She hadn't appreciated Taylor's response. When Taylor dismissed Kate's feelings, no matter how hurtful that was to Kate, Kate knew that meant her friend's mind was set on accomplishing something, no matter how illogical it was. She was brave even when her ideas lacked common sense.

In this case, Kate needed to be either all in or remove herself from the situation. Although she'd love to walk away from the crazy scheme, her loyalty to her friend won. She wished she had the ability to stand up and say "no," but to complicate things, Lacey was involved. Kate had enough problems with Lacey at school that she didn't want to add to them. She decided to go along with the plan and prayed that everything worked out well in the end. But how much trouble would they get into when the plan fell apart? Kate cringed. She didn't want to find out.

CHAPTER SIX

The next day the girls saddled their horses and rode again to the old barn. They had some serious cleaning to do. This time, though, Kate brought a surgical mask to protect her lungs from the dust. She'd feel stupid wearing it but it was better than having to explain to her mother why she was having another asthma attack like the one she'd had last night. She managed to convince her mom that it was caused by dusting a stall, which was partially true, but no way would her mother buy that excuse twice. Prevention was the only way.

Taylor, the determined one, had walked over earlier and brought two brooms, borrowed from the main barn, a hammer and nails, and old towels. Their plan last night to meet again, to bring the supplies and to start cleaning, had fallen through due to Kate's asthma attack and Taylor's surprise dinner plans with her family.

They needed to ride daily anyway, and the fastest way to cause suspicion would be for them not to ride. With that thought in mind, they said they were going on a trail ride today.

The girls dismounted, tying their horses to trees with halters they'd packed, and one by one they entered the barn.

"I noticed some missing nails, so I'm going to fix a few things," Taylor said, holding up the hammer like she was a tough woman with muscle power. She actually was the toughest girl Kate had ever met.

"I'll sweep the aisle in the barn since Kate's allergic to dust," Lacey offered. "I'd recommend staying out of the barn until the dust settles," she said to Kate.

That was thoughtful of Lacey. Maybe she wasn't so bad after all. "I'll start pulling down vines from the outside wall," Kate said, pulling from her pocket a pair of flowered work gloves that she borrowed from her parents' shed. Her mother loved gardening and yard work. Kate had decided the vines needed to be removed.

"You have quite a job ahead of you," Lacey said to Kate. "We'll help you once we're finished with our jobs in the barn."

"Thanks. I think the most important part is to remove the vines by Thunder's window so he's safe," Kate explained. "We need to decide which stall we want him to use."

"How about that one?" Lacey pointed to a weathered stall, the first one on the right. "It has less vines and the door to close the window is intact."

"Perfect." Kate slid the stall door open to make her way through his stall. She opened the half doors and squinted when a stream of light flooded the dark stall. Lacey was right; the doors were intact and in good shape. She stepped through the narrow doorway and into the small paddock. The vines weren't too thick. It would be a job to remove them but the other stalls were covered and would be almost impossible to remove. She stuck her hands in the flowered gloves, and as if her mother were there, her presence enveloped Kate. Maybe her mom was supporting her without knowing, but more likely, she was telling her to walk away and stop the nonsense before she started. Kate hesitated, wanting to listen, wanting to follow her advice, but then she saw Tayler and Lacey heading into the barn carrying supplies. Peer pressure was a horrible thing.

Kate grabbed a handful of vine and ripped it from the wall. The vine stuck to the boards like a bird's claws, grasping for life to cling to something solid. She yanked harder and the vine broke free. It pulled off in a long, curly mess. This was going to be a big project. The vine took more effort to remove than Kate had thought. She tried to tug it out of the ground but it was deeply embedded and wouldn't budge. For the time being, she decided to leave it in one piece even though it was still alive and intact. At least it was pulled away from the window. The goal was to remove it away from the opening for his safety, and she'd accomplished that.

She reached as high as possible and started pulling another vine. The dang thing was stubborn. There were little runners off the main stem that buried themselves deep into the grooves of the barn. She pulled hard and the top of it loosened enough from the wood that she was able to work it enough that it released its hold. She tugged until the strand of vine came loose from the barn except for the root. She placed it on top of the prior one.

An hour later she was still pulling vines into a pile when she stopped to study her progress. The barn looked much cleaner, at least this section, but she still had over halfway to go before the area would be safe for Thunder. Poor horse. He was homeless, and they were about to isolate him more by hiding him in a barn by himself. She hoped he wouldn't be lonely. Horses thrived from being around other horses. At least if they kept open the window he'd be able to see old man Brown's horses grazing in the pasture. Honestly, Thunder deserved to graze in a large pasture too, instead of being hidden in someone's barn.

Kate knew about being alone. Her family was always busy and Kate often missed her parents. Her father worked a lot and even though her mother didn't formally work, she volunteered for several different organizations. While that was caring of her mother to help others, Kate was tired of staying home alone. Sometimes she enjoyed the quiet, but when it became too much, she'd find herself at Taylor's house, which was almost always noisy with two younger twins.

Someone sneezed loudly from inside the barn. Kate could only imagine the amount of dust floating around caused by Lacey's sweeping. She was grateful to be outside pulling vines no matter how hard they were to tear off the barn.

She wished she had music to listen to. Everyone else her age had a cell phone, an endless supply of music, but her mother refused to allow her to own one. That was yet another thing that made her feel different from the other kids. They texted and socialized with each other but Kate was excluded from that scene. Of course, that was her mother's point. She preached that social media was dangerous and that Kate didn't need exposure to an unmonitored, scary world. Kate disagreed. Didn't her mother trust her? Of course she did, Kate argued with herself. But cell phones were about more than talking to strangers and having access to the Internet; it was a connection to her friends. That was an argument her mother didn't understand.

To entertain herself, Kate started to hum. If she didn't have music she'd make her own. It helped pass the time.

Before long Lacey poked her head out of Thunder's new stall door to talk to Kate. "Don't go in there until the dust settles, but it's much cleaner. You'll love it."

"I can't wait to see it," Kate said. They were making wonderful progress on the barn and one step closer to bringing Thunder here. Kate wasn't sure she should be excited.

"Wow! His window looks amazing." Lacey stood next to Kate now, admiring the clean barn wall.

"I can't pull the roots out of the ground; they are alive. I piled them up." Kate pointed to the mound of roots next to her.

Lacey shrugged. "I don't think it matters. It's not like Thunder will live here forever."

That brought up a more important question. "What's the bigger plan?" Kate asked. "Thunder can't stay here forever. I mean, someone will eventually discover him."

"To find his owners. This buys us more time to figure out where he's from," Lacey said with certainty.

"And if we don't?"

"We will." Lacey's voice held so much

confidence that Kate almost believed her.

"I don't mean to be a downer," Kate said, "but we've had no calls yet from our fliers."

"If not, then we can find him a good home." Lacey leaned against the section of the barn that Kate had cleaned. "We'll have a say in where he goes. With the rescue, they pick who takes him. I don't like that."

Kate agreed with her. "Finding a home for him will be hard without connections." She wasn't trying to change their minds, but she did want to point out the obstacles they'd be sure to face.

Lacey wasn't interested in hearing roadblocks. "We'll figure it out."

Kate gave up and yanked on another vine until it loosened its grasp. A straggly line of vine unwound from the barn. She piled it with the others.

"I'd love to paint this barn," Lacey said. "Maybe with a fresh coat of red paint. Too bad old man Brown doesn't fix it up."

Kate gazed at the barn. The old red paint, replaced by a fresh coat, would make a huge difference in appearance. She could easily imagine the dingy trim painted white around the windows, the rusty tin roof replaced with a shiny one, and the dirt floors of the stalls lined with mats and filled with fresh shavings. "I'd love to own this barn," Kate said. "Mr. Brown doesn't realize how lucky he is to have this prize."

"He has a new barn practically outside his door, so he doesn't need one down the hill and hidden in the woods. What a shame," Lacey added.

Taylor appeared from around the corner of the barn. "I fixed the most crucial boards until I ran out of nails. I'll bring some more tomorrow." Taylor glanced over Kate's work. "Good job. If we work on this more after school tomorrow, I bet we can sneak Thunder out tomorrow evening once it gets dark."

Tomorrow evening. The thought made Kate's mind swirl around in fast circles. She reminded herself that she was committed to the wild adventure with her friends, so she needed to keep her mouth shut and agree, no matter the cost.

"Kate?" Taylor asked, poking her toe into the pile of live vines by the bush. "Are you okay with the plan?"

Now was her chance to tell her exactly what she thought. Kate looked up at Lacey instead of Taylor. Miss Popular would spread the word at school if Kate admitted she was afraid. Sam would find out, her other friends would too, and people would laugh at her. The worst thing in the world was to have no friends at lunch to sit with. No, she wouldn't say a word other than to agree.

"I'm fine," was all Kate managed to say.

"Let's help Kate finish removing the vines from the window and then call it an afternoon,"

Taylor said. "We'll meet back here tomorrow to finish." She turned to Lacey. "Can you have your friend buy some hay, shavings and feed? If they'll keep a secret, have them drop the supplies off tomorrow afternoon where the street and the beginning of the wagon road meet. Maybe hide everything behind the bushes, and we can carry them down the wagon road and inside the barn to the tack room."

"I already asked and she agreed to help us," Lacey said, grabbing hold of a thick vine and tugging. "I'll go with her when school is finished."

"Kate, can you scrub out two water buckets, grab some hooks from the main barn, and carry them down here after school?" Taylor asked. "I'm going to finish the barn repairs."

"Sure." That was easy enough. It was the part about tomorrow night, relocating Thunder, that concerned her.

CHAPTER SEVEN

Tomorrow afternoon came too quickly for Kate. Usually school dragged by, lasting forever it seemed, but today school was over almost before it started. Kate wanted to skip today altogether.

Reluctantly she stepped from the safety of her mother's car and into the barn parking lot. All she had to do was to scrub two buckets and carry them over to old man Brown's barn. That was simple enough. Right? Who was she kidding? She was scared to participate on any level in Taylor's adventure.

Pushing the worry from her mind, or at least trying, she walked into the main barn's tack room to look for extra water buckets. The room was organized, thanks to Layne's amazing skills, and Kate found a stack of buckets in the far corner. She picked two navy ones, and to her surprise, they were clean. They even had hooks on them.

Mystery Horse

Kate poked her head out of the tack room, making sure no one was around before she smuggled them to the smaller barn. Little Candice turned the corner, almost bumping into Kate.

"Hi, Kate!" Candice exclaimed. "Want to ride together?"

Her younger friend was adorable and Kate hated to say no, but she didn't have time to ride. They had a lot of preparation left to do for Thunder's departure tonight. "I wasn't planning on riding," Kate explained. "I will tomorrow, though." Kate hoped she wasn't making a promise she'd have to break. She didn't know how much was involved with taking care of Thunder, but the truth was she needed to ride Razor. All this "trail riding" wasn't enough to keep Razor fit and calm. He was a horse that needed to be worked several days a week due to his higher energy level.

"What are you doing?" Candice glanced at the water buckets in Kate's hand.

Kate wasn't about to start lying to her friends. Withholding information was a form of lying, Kate was well aware of, but she wasn't about to dump unnecessary information on Candice. Friends didn't do that to one another.

"Nothing. I'm only here for a few minutes." Kate decided to avoid the real question at hand.

"I miss riding with the Horse Club. When are we having another meeting?"

Kate had no idea. They'd been so focused on Thunder lately that having a meeting to discuss rules or ways to help out the community hadn't entered their minds. "Maybe next week. We've been so busy helping with Thunder we haven't done much else." That was the honest truth.

"Layne said he's leaving tomorrow morning," Candice said. "Too bad. He's a good looking horse."

"That he is." Kate leaned against the tack room doorframe. She was tired from all the work she'd done yesterday pulling vines. Her shoulders hurt, even her thighs ached.

"I was hoping someone from the barn would keep him," Candice said. "He seems well trained. I bet he's been to shows before."

Kate had wondered the same thing.

"Too bad Lacey doesn't keep him," Candice continued.

Lacey? That thought had never occurred to Kate. "Why Lacey?" she asked out of curiosity.

"Blue has been lame. Besides, she needs a bigger horse anyway." Candice pulled her hair back in a pony tail, preparing to ride.

Kate realized she was blocking the tack room door. She thought Candice was holding her up but in reality it was the other way around. "Oh, I'm sorry." Kate stepped aside to allow Candice to step into the room. "I didn't realize I was blocking you."

"No worries." Candice danced past Kate. She pulled out her saddle, pad, and bridle from her locker. "Anyway, I hope Thunder goes to a good home."

Little did Candice know where Thunder was headed. Kate didn't consider old man Brown's barn a good home, filled with love, other horses, and green pastures, but tonight he'd be hidden there.

Taylor was probably waiting for Kate to show up with the buckets. "See you later," she called out to Candice. Kate hurried out of the barn with the buckets. Thankfully she didn't run into anyone else.

The trail was much longer on foot than when she rode Razor. She tried to memorize it as best she could, so tonight, when it was dark outside, she'd know where the dips and turns were in the trail. A flashlight was only so good at highlighting a path. It took about twenty minutes to reach the old barn. Taylor was there but Lacey was no where to be found.

Taylor looked up. She had a nail hanging from her lips and a hammer in her hand. She was working on the window door outside Thunder's new stall.

"I was getting worried about you," Taylor said with a muffled voice from the nail between her lips. She removed the nail, pounded it into the frame of the window, and then turned her full attention to Kate.

"I got held up talking to Candice. She wanted to ride," Kate explained.

Taylor's eyebrows lifted. "How did you get out of that one?"

"I promised to ride tomorrow." Kate looked inside the window to see if Lacey was in the barn.

Taylor understood, glancing at her watch. "Lacey is supposed to meet us at the beginning of the old wagon road in about ten minutes."

The supplies. They'd have to carry the heavy items down the dirt road and to the old barn. If Kate thought she was sore now, tomorrow promised to be worse.

"Too bad I didn't think to bring a wheelbarrow, but I'm sure someone would have noticed me heading across the parking lot with it," Kate said. She wished they had one to make the task easier.

"Yeah, I'm sure Layne would have noticed." Taylor knocked another nail into the trim and said, "I'm finished here. Let's walk down the road and meet her." She set the hammer on a stump next to a box of nails.

They walked down the dirt road in silence, each of them contemplating the upcoming adventure. When they reached the street, Lacey wasn't there yet.

Kate didn't speak but found a log to sit on and wait. She hoped everything was going as planned with Lacey and her friend. Kate hated to get another person involved in their scheme but they had no choice. None of them had a driver's license so they had to rely on someone else.

They waited for at least twenty minutes before Taylor spoke. "Wonder where they are?"

Before Kate answered, a dented pickup truck rumbled down the street and parked in front of them. The first thing Kate noticed was it needed to be washed badly. It was supposed to be silver but a layer of dirt covered it. Someone had written the words "Wash Me" on the passenger door. Lacey swung open the door, climbed from the worn seat, and then walked to the backside of the truck. She lowered the tailgate, tossing a bale of hay onto the ground.

Kate hopped up from the log she was sitting on. There was no turning back now.

"Hang on and we'll help," Taylor said, standing up.

They joined Lacey and her friend, who had climbed into the back of the truck. Kate had seen the girl at school before, she ate lunch at Lacey's table, but Kate didn't know her name. Maybe it was best she didn't, so when they were busted for this crazy scheme, and when the adults wanted to know who was involved, the girl would stay out of trouble. The girl, wearing her straight hair pulled back to keep it out of her eyes, tossed the plastic-wrapped bales of shavings over the side of the truck. When she finished, she handed Taylor a bag of feed. Lacey had chosen the same kind of feed Layne used, which was a smart choice. It was never a good idea to abruptly change a horse's diet.

When all the supplies were lying on the ground next to the truck, they thanked the girl before she drove off. The three of them stood still, staring at the pile.

"I should have asked her to drive down the wagon road but I didn't want old man Brown to see the truck," Lacey said.

"Good call," Taylor said. "Let's hide the supplies behind that bush until we can carry it all to the barn." She pointed toward a mangle of shrubs on the nearside of the wagon road. They worked together to move the items from view.

Taylor grabbed the twine of the last remaining bale of hay still sitting on the side of the road. "Kate, can you pick up the other end and help me carry this to the barn?"

Kate slid her hands under the twine and grabbed on. She wished she had thought to bring her mother's gardening gloves because the twine dug into her fingers from the weight of the bale. With the two of them lifting together the bale was manageable but they had to set it down several times to rest.

"The road is longer than I thought," Kate complained.

"No kidding," Taylor agreed.

Lacey struggled with one of the bags of shavings. From the strained look on her face she was having a difficult time too.

"Who's idea was this?" Kate joked.

Taylor glared at her. "You agreed."

Kate scowled at her friend. So that was the way it was going to be. When the crazy plan blew up in their faces, and it would blow up, Kate could almost hear those words repeated. *You agreed.* Some friend she was.

"I was joking," Kate said, defending herself. "I was talking about carrying this heavy stuff not about hiding Thunder." Although both ideas sounded horrible at the moment.

"No one ever just jokes," Taylor said with an edge in her voice. She let go of her end of the hay. The twine cut into Kate's hands, causing her to drop the bale, which landed in the dirt. "People joke about what they're really thinking."

Maybe there was truth in that logic.

"We're in this together," Taylor said.

"That's right. We are, so lose the defensive attitude," Kate said, fed up with Taylor's prickly, pushy behavior.

"Come on," Lacey said, resting one end of the heavy bag on the ground. "We have a long night ahead of us. Let it go."

Lacey was right. They needed to be a team if

they were going to pull this off. "I'm sorry. I thought adding humor to the situation was a good idea. I was wrong."

"I'd say," Taylor snapped. "But thanks for the apology." She picked up her end of the hay again and waited for Kate to grab hold of hers.

Kate hesitated. She rubbed her sore hand. "Next time warn me before you let go," Kate said. "That hurt.

"Sorry." Taylor frowned.

Taylor seemed sincere enough, so Kate picked up her end of the bale.

"We're almost there," Lacey encouraged. "Then I suggest we take a break. I packed a few bottles of water and some granola bars."

"You're my new best friend," Taylor said lightly.

Kate flashed her a look. Really? Her new best friend? What did that make Kate? She decided she was feeling testy due to nerves and fatigue. It was hard work carrying a bale of hay down the long road, especially after all the physical labor they did on the barn yesterday. Her body still hadn't recovered. She had new appreciation for all the yard work her mother did around the house to beautify the garden and lawn. Unfortunately, she wasn't able to share her gratitude with her mother.

Kate had been so tired last night that she'd gone to bed early. She'd slept through the night without so much as a dream. Her mother questioned the early bedtime but Kate shrugged it off. Her mother blamed it on the unpredictability and moodiness of Kate's age. Kate didn't correct her.

The barn was in sight and Kate's shoulders were on fire. "I need to put the bale down for a minute."

Taylor kept walking.

Kate wasn't in the mood to battle with her stubborn, independent friend. "I'm setting this down." She gave Taylor a moment to listen, and then she let go of the twine.

"Ouch! That hurt," Taylor complained.

"Tell me about it. At least I warned you."

Lacey placed the bag of shavings down next to them. "Stop it. Both of you," she commanded. "I've heard enough to last the rest of tonight."

The girls stopped arguing. No one said a word, and Kate sat on the edge of the bale of hay to rest.

"We need to keep going," Lacey said. "We have a lot to do before dinnertime."

Again, Lacey was right.

Kate stood up, slipping her hand back under the twine. She waited for Taylor to join her and together they picked up the bale of hay. Kate had had enough of carrying it to the barn, but she didn't dare voice her complaint. She bit back the sarcastic comments that swirled in her mind. She needed to get through this task, so they could leave and return home, even if for a short time before they had to meet back at the barn.

The last ten feet of carrying the hay was the hardest. It should have been easier, with the ending in sight, but it wasn't. She breathed deeply to force herself to make it to the tack room. When they reached it, she let out a long sigh and rubbed her sore hands together.

"We made it," Lacey said in her cheerleader voice. There was no question as to why she was selected to be on the cheerleading squad at school; she excelled at pumping up one's mood when she wanted to.

"We have another bale of hay and a couple more bags of shavings to carry." Taylor groaned.

Kate was relieved that she wasn't the only one feeling the pain.

"Break time first," Kate said, walking outside to sit on a stump. "I don't think my muscles will tolerate lifting anything else until I rest. They are shaking."

"Mine too," Taylor said. It was nice they agreed on something after all their bickering.

Kate's mom always said the fix to any negative situation was to inject positive comments into the equation. Kate decided she'd give it a try.

"You did a great job buying all the supplies," Kate told Lacey. "I'm glad your friend agreed."

Lacey beamed from the compliment. "Thanks,

Kate. She's my best friend and promised not to tell anyone." Lacey dumped out the contents of her backpack and passed out the snack.

"You know, we're all doing a good job," Taylor said, jumping on the positive-feedback game, which is what Kate's mom named it.

"We've made a lot of progress in a short amount of time," Kate said. "Take the barn for instance. It looks like a different building."

Taylor grinned.

Voices carried from somewhere down the path.

"Shhhh," Kate whispered. "Someone's on the wagon trail."

Taylor slowly stood. "We need to hide inside the barn. They're headed this way." She quickly shoved their snack back into Lacey's backpack. They hurried into the barn with Kate and Lacey following closely behind. Who was on the trail? Had old man Brown seen them carrying the supplies to his barn? Had they made too much noise with all their arguing?

CHAPTER EIGHT

The voices grew louder. Someone was walking down the wagon trail and heading toward the barn.

The three girls hid in Thunder's new stall. Taylor peeked out from the corner of the window.

"Who is it?" Kate whispered.

"I don't know," Taylor said in such a quiet voice that Kate struggled to make out the words.

Sure enough, the voices grew louder.

Taylor ducked. She placed her finger over her mouth to warn the girls not to talk. Someone was outside the barn. If it was old man Brown, he'd wonder who cleaned up his barn. If he came inside to explore, the girls would be trapped in the stall.

Thankfully they had carried the supplies earlier into the feed room and closed the door. Then Kate remembered the items hidden behind the bushes at the beginning of the road. Were they hidden well enough?

The girls remained silent. After a few long moments, Taylor peeked out the window again. She gasped. She lowered herself down until she was right in front of Kate and Lacey.

"It's Candice and a couple of other girls on horseback," Taylor whispered.

Kate remembered that Candice was planning to ride. They were most likely cooling out their horses afterward by walking on the wagon trail.

The kids didn't seem to notice that the barn was mysteriously cleaned up. They rode past, chatting about school. When they disappeared around the bend by Mr. Brown's house, the girls stood to stretch their aching legs.

"That was close," Taylor said.

"I didn't know anyone else rode down here," Kate said. "What are we going to do once Thunder is here? He'll hear them coming down the road and will look out the window. He might even call out to them."

Taylor frowned. "I guess I thought we were the only ones who ventured down this trail."

"That was a fluke," Lacey said in her reassuring tone. "I don't think most people come this far off the main path."

"My guess is Candice showed her friends the trail because she's ridden here with us," Kate said. "We rarely ride here, so maybe they'll pick a different path next time."

Taylor leaned against the wall with a strung-out expression on her face. "I hope that's the case. I'm glad we weren't carrying supplies down the road when they rode by."

Kate shuddered at the thought. "I wonder if they'll come back this way." The trail continued past Mr. Brown's house but it led to a fairly busy road. Sometimes they didn't want to take the long way around, so they would double back on the wagon trail to return to the barn.

Taylor lifted her eyebrows. "Good point. The supplies are hidden well from the street, but not so well from the trail. They might easily notice them."

"We need to get the supplies before it gets dark," Lacey added. "If we try now, and they turn back, they'll see us."

"What do we do?" Kate asked.

Taylor wiggled her leg back and forth as she leaned against the stall. "Lacey's right. We don't have time to carry the items down the road. I think we should hide them better."

"We need to hurry," Kate said, her belly in a nervous knot. She hated all this stress.

"Let's go," Taylor said, pushing off the wall and heading toward the stall door. Kate and Lacey were right behind her.

They made it to the end of the wagon road much quicker than when they were struggling with the supplies earlier. There was no sign of the girls, but that didn't mean they wouldn't come back. They reached the bush and moved the items as quickly as possible underneath the shrubs to hide them better.

"That should do it for now," Taylor said, wiping saw dust, which escaped a small hole from the bag, off her hands and riding pants.

Kate heard voices again. "That's them!"

The girls looked for a place to hide.

"Follow me," Taylor said quietly but with urgency in her voice. She scurried under the bush and folded herself next to a bag of shavings. Lacey scooted under the opening in the bush and practically sat on top of Taylor, who grunted in protest, but Lacey didn't move. Kate joined them, squashing herself into the side of another bag of shavings.

"Stay still," Taylor whispered.

The horses headed toward the girls. Kate prayed that the prickly leaves on the bush were enough to hide them. Speaking of prickly things, Kate did her best to ignore a sharp branch pushing into the middle of her back. She didn't dare move.

Spirit stopped in his tracks, staring right at the girls. He snorted and planted his feet, refusing to move forward.

"Oh, silly pony," Candice said. "There's nothing there. Get going."

The pony remained frozen.

Candice kicked him harder but Spirit didn't move.

"You go in front of me," Candice said to another girl. "He thinks he sees the boogeyman." She laughed.

Little did Candice know, Spirit did sense something. Kate held her breath. If they sat still she hoped the pony would move past them.

Candice's friend urged her horse forward and he walked past the hidden girls. The horse was staring at them, snorting, but he passed by them. Candice kicked Spirit again and the pony followed his friend, although with hesitancy. None of the three girls in the bush moved much less barely breathed. When the horses walked by, Kate let out a long sigh.

"No kidding," Taylor said, answering Kate's sigh. "That was nerve wracking."

"At least we can carry the rest of the supplies to the barn without worrying about the girls," Kate said. She grabbed hold of the bag of shavings in front of her, and while bent over to avoid the overhead branches, she dragged out the bag from underneath the straggly branch. It caught on a thorn and ripped another hole in the plastic. She had to wiggle the bag and push on the branch until it was free.

Lacey joined her by grabbing another bag of shavings. Taylor surfaced from the opening in the bush with the last item, a bale of hay. Kate had no idea how Taylor would manage the hay alone but her friend dragged it behind her.

Ready to finish the chore of carrying the supplies back to the old barn, none of them complained. Kate was silent because the thought of removing Thunder from the barn tonight occupied her mind. They would each return home to eat dinner, and then once it turned dark, they'd meet at the big barn for their horse adventur

CHAPTER NINE

"Don't you like your dinner?" Kate's mom asked.

Kate slid the food around her plate. Her mother had made steak, Kate's favorite, a baked potato with sour cream, another of Kate's favorites, steamed green beans, and a salad of greens. It was just the two of them eating dinner together. Kate's dad was working late again.

"I love it, Mom." Kate appreciated that her mother cooked for the two of them but Kate's belly was tied in knots. Her emotions were moving from guilt to fear, and back again. The girls were about to take a huge step toward independence, if that's what she wanted to call it, but once they had Thunder in their possession, he was their responsibility.

She studied her mom's innocent face. The woman had no idea what was about to happen. Guilt jabbed at Kate's heart, causing her to turn her head away from her mother.

"What's with you tonight?" her mom asked with concern in her voice. "You aren't acting like yourself."

"I'm fine," Kate snapped. She hadn't meant to use that tone with her mother but the stress was getting to her.

Her mother stared at her from across the dinner table. "Kate, that's enough. If you don't want to share what's bothering you, then so be it, but don't take your frustration out on me."

Kate chose not to answer verbally. Instead she pushed her plate aside, answer enough. She hated wasting food that her mother had prepared, but her stomach rejected the thought of eating. The one bite of steak she'd already eaten sat like a chunk of lead in her belly.

"I'm sorry, Mom, but I can't eat."

"Are you sick? Maybe you need to head to bed early tonight," her mother suggested. Even though her eyebrows were raised in question, Kate knew she was concerned.

An early bedtime was a perfect excuse to hide away until dark, and her mother would never know she was missing unless she checked on her later. Kate's stomach knotted again. What would she do if her mother opened her door to say goodnight and Kate wasn't in her bed?

Don't panic.

Kate reminded herself to stay calm. Her dad

always preached that nothing good happened in situations if people reacted emotionally instead of thinking their options through. With his profession as a doctor, he had no choice but to remain calm during a crisis.

"Kate?" her mom asked as she tapped Kate's arm. "Your mind is far away. What are you worried about?"

Kate wished it were possible to tell her. She didn't enjoy keeping secrets from her parents, or from anyone for that matter.

"An early bedtime?" her mom asked again.

Kate avoided looking at her but nodded. That was the best she could offer without flat out lying.

She resented Taylor for putting her in a position where honesty was impossible. Kate suspected that in this situation her father would say that Kate was responsible for telling the truth and any lies were her decision. She supposed he was right. Taylor wasn't at fault, Kate was, for agreeing to the plan from the beginning. Unless she backed out before tonight.

In general, her father's wisdom was great but it was confusing at the moment. Her friends were counting on her. Peer pressure once again. Sometimes Kate wished she could skip being a preteen and fast forward to being in college. Life would be easier then.

Kate carried her full plate to the sink. While

she needed to eat to gain strength to accomplish what she had to do tonight, not to mention all the work she'd done the past two days, she settled for packing a snack, instead.

"Don't throw that away," her mother commanded from her seat.

Kate pulled out of the cabinet a glass bowl with a plastic snap lid and scraped her dinner into it. She'd eat it later, when she returned after tonight's awful adventure if she found herself hungry. If not, she had lunch for tomorrow. Either way she'd make sure she ate what her mother had cooked.

"Night," she said, kissing her mom on the cheek. If one of Kate's friends had been around, kissing her mother would have been out of the question. She suspected at some point she'd have to give up the practice altogether. But honest to God? She loved hugging and kissing her mother goodnight.

"I didn't mean bed this early," her mother said.

"I know, but it's a good idea." Kate headed for the stairs. Before she placed her foot on the bottom step, she looked back at her mother, who was still sitting at the table. Kate's life was about to change, and the event tonight would mark the beginning of her independence. "Love you, Mom," Kate managed to say.

"Love you too," her mom called back. "Just remember, whatever is bothering you won't last forever. A month from now you won't even remember your problem."

Her mother was wrong on that point. She was fairly certain she'd remember tonight for the rest of her life.

Kate went upstairs to her room and closed the door. Shaggy Dog, the overstuffed animal she'd had since she was five-years old, waited for her on her pillow. Kate scooped the stuffed animal into her arms and collapsed onto her bed. If she called Taylor, her mom might overhear the conversation, or Kate might get cold feet and back out of the plan. Again, Kate wished it were that easy to back out. Kate imagined picking up the phone and telling Taylor she'd changed her mind. Just the thought of the confrontation with her friend made her stomach knot more.

What was the worst thing that could happen if Kate cancelled? So what, Taylor would get upset, say some hurtful words. Was that all? Not even close. Taylor, or worse yet, Lacey, would go to school Monday and whisper behind her back. She'd tell everyone how Kate had backed out of a dare at the last minute because she was scared. They'd call her a baby, laugh at her. The vision of sitting at lunch alone resurfaced. That was death in itself.

She had no choice but to follow through with the dumb plan.

Thunder popped into her mind. Was it so bad if

he went to a rescue? As if to answer the question, she had a disturbing vision of him being in a barn full of unwanted horses. There were so many horses that no one brought him carrots or brushed him. She'd seen his mane knotted and his coat covered in mud when he first arrived, and in her vision he looked like that again, only worse. There were no girls to love him, to hand graze him on a strip of grass daily. He'd get skinny.

Thunder deserved a girl to adopt him, love him, ride him. She envisioned him in horse shows jumping over fences and winning blue ribbons. He'd have his own show attire, set of winter blankets, and grooming supplies. He deserved a girl to groom him until his coat shined. Yes, he did indeed.

Who were they to stand in his way of happiness? He needed to return home.

Kate crawled under a fuzzy brown and white horse blanket she'd gotten for Christmas last year and stared out the window, thinking about Thunder. The full moon was rising, and before long it would light the path to the barn, no flashlight needed. That was when she'd make her silent escape, when her decision would impact her life forever.

Kate drifted off to sleep. When she awoke she was disoriented and anxious. Where was she? She glanced around, absorbing the instant familiarity of her room. She'd had a wild dream that she was in a jungle running for her life.

The moon beamed into her room and lit up her bed. She jolted upright.

Thunder!

She glanced at the clock. She was supposed to meet Taylor and Lacey twenty minutes ago! With her heart pounding, she slid from the comfort of her bed. Just before she grabbed hold of the doorknob to experience the biggest adventure of her life, she thought to shove two pillows under the covers to make it look as though she were lying in bed in case her mother decided to glance into the room. As an afterthought, and probably hesitation to leave the safety of her room, she took her time pulling on a lightweight jacket. Inhaling a long breath to calm her nerves, she found enough bravery to crack open her bedroom door to evaluate where her parents were. The house was quiet. Too quiet.

She tiptoed into the hallway, crept down the steps, and when no one stopped her, she slipped out the side door. Her friends were probably wondering where she was, and because she didn't have a cell phone, it wasn't as though they could call her to find out.

She hurried down the street, making an effort to stay in the shadows to avoid the light from the full moon, and crossed through a neighbor's yard. The trail head would lead to the main barn. She picked her way over tree roots and around large rocks, but barely down the trail, a piercing bark rang out in the night. She tried to ignore the animal staring out the family-room door and picked up her pace. She hoped the owner of the dog wouldn't glance outside and discover her. Again, she made a point to stay in the shadows, but it wasn't always possible. She was out in the open at the moment. The moon was so bright that if someone looked out the window they'd see her easily. With luck she'd soon be hidden by the woods.

Kate heard a sliding door open. The dog busted through the opening and bolted toward her. Kate shrieked. Thank goodness the dog stopped short of the path due to an invisible fence. If Kate thought her heart was pounding before, it was off the chart now. She wasn't cut out for this kind of adventure.

"Who's out there?" a woman called.

Kate didn't dare answer. The path ahead was in full moonlight and if the dog continued to bark, the lady would walk outside to explore. Kate just wanted to get away. No longer caring if the woman saw her she hurried forward. The moonlight was bright but it was difficult to navigate. She tripped over a root and almost fell. The dog's bark turned to a low growl.

Oh, please don't run through the invisible fence.

Kate hurried down the path. She crossed over the grass-covered bridge of the narrow creek and up the hill toward the main barn. Off in the distance she heard the dog barking. The woman was likely still calling out to see who was there, but Kate could no longer hear her.

She reached the main barn finally. No one was there! Thunder was missing from his stall, and the barn was eerily quiet.

Taylor and Lacey had left without her. She didn't blame them, and part of her was relieved that she hadn't actually participated in the act of smuggling Thunder out of the barn, but worry quickly replaced the temporary relief. They'd be mad at her, for sure.

Mostly unfamiliar with the overgrown trail to old man Brown's barn, she set out on the dark path.

CHAPTER TEN

Kate walked the trail as fast as the rough terrain allowed. She half expected to run into Thunder and her friends on the path but they were nowhere to be found. Taylor probably waited at the barn for ten minutes before she gave up and continued on with the plan. It was likely they weren't that far ahead of her on the trail. They'd have to walk slower while leading Thunder on the rough path, though as far as Kate understood, horses had better night vision than humans did.

If she considered the fact she was walking quickly, they might be five minutes ahead of her on the trail. Kate picked up her pace a bit but when she slipped on a stick and almost fell, she slowed down again. It wasn't worth falling. If anything, she'd catch up with them at old man Brown's barn.

The trail looked different at night on foot. She didn't remember the bend up ahead, nor did she remember crossing the creek at another grassy bridge. Had she missed the turnoff?

The path was lit well, but there were darker sections deeper in the woods where it was harder to see the trail. Maybe Kate missed the wagon road. In a hurry, she decided not to waste time by turning back in case she was on the right path.

At least five minutes down the path she had no clue where she was. There was a huge, unfamiliar house on the right side and woods on the left with a gazebo in a small clearing. Kate was sure she'd never passed by the house before when riding on the wagon road. Had she missed the turnoff?

Concerned, she glanced back in the direction she'd walked. The last thing she wanted was to explore the woods at night, alone, and lost. Suddenly she missed her friends and Thunder. Where was she?

Fear swirled around her belly and the knot from earlier was bigger now. Not only would her friends be angry at her, the cause of some of her fear and anxiety, but she was afraid of the dark. Here she was, out in the woods by herself, late at night. She'd heard stories of coyotes roaming the area. As the saying went, they attacked people, especially kids, and even horses.

A chill ran down her spine.

She turned around and travelled in the direction she came from. As far as she remembered, there had been no turnoffs from the trail, so she needed to pay closer attention if she wanted to find the wagon road. Too bad she hadn't brought a flashlight.

As if the moon heard her doubts and wanted to play off them, it hid behind a dense cloud, and what bright light she'd had, disappeared. Tears clouded her vision and a lump formed in her throat. Right now she didn't care if she cried. No one would know, and if they did, so what, even adults cry.

Kate stopped in her tracks, mostly because she couldn't see where to place her feet. She looked up at the dark sky. *Please help me find my friends. I know I didn't want to be included in this scheme, and you made that happen to an extent, but right now I'm scared. Please keep me safe. Please let the moonlight brighten my way.*

As if her prayer was answered the moon slid out from the clouds and lit the path. Maybe she should have prayed earlier, then she wouldn't be lost.

She continued to walk, still not recognizing where she was. At some point, Taylor and she had ridden every trail in their neighborhood, but for some reason it looked completely different at night. She kept a close eye on the right side of the path, certain that was the side the old wagon trail was on, determined to find it.

Kate walked longer than she imagined. There wasn't another trail anywhere. She crossed back over the bridge and had to be heading in the correct direction. It was the only way she could go.

After another five minutes the trail spilled out onto a road. There were no signs to identify the street and there was nothing recognizable. She had no clue where she was.

***

Taylor held on tight to Thunder's lead rope. He was spooking at every little thing. Apparently he'd never been on a trail at night. Most horses haven't. But he was overreacting and jumping at every little noise, every tiny movement in the woods, even imaginary ones.

Taylor remembered how they hid in the bushes earlier from Candice and her friends. The horses had sensed they were there. They either smelled them, saw them, or heard them, she didn't know. One thing was for certain, though, they knew someone was hiding in the bushes. What if Thunder was overreacting for a reason? Could someone, or something, be hiding in the woods watching them, ready to attack?

The thought made her clench her hands tighter around his lead rope.

Lacey was jabbering on as if nothing was of concern. Perhaps she didn't realize how nervous Thunder was because she wasn't the one leading him. And that was another thing. She should have thought to bring a flashlight. She hadn't counted on the moon disappearing behind the clouds on and off, leaving the path dark and almost impassable.

Taylor was supposed to be the brave one, or so everyone thought. Well, she had fears too. People always thought she was older than she was, often forgetting she was a kid with real life fears. Part of that was her own fault. Usually she hid her uncertainties from people because she wasn't comfortable letting her weaker side show. She didn't know why she was like that, she just was. The more she thought about things, the more she realized that hiding her fears might have to do with being the oldest kid in the family and having younger twins for siblings. She had a lot of responsibility. Her mother always asked for her help, from changing diapers early on to babysitting, allowing her mother to run a quick errand to the grocery store. Taylor developed the habit of pretending to act older than she was, taking on chores such as helping to cook dinner and clean house. She was always the strong one. All Taylor's friends went to her during stressful times and she was the one who solved their problems. That kind of pressure caused her not to want to appear weak or unable to handle situations.

Thunder snorted at a branch hanging over the trail. "What do you think that is, Thunder? I mean, come on." Taylor cued him forward but he was determined that the branch wanted to attack him.

Lacey kept talking. Taylor had no clue what she was even jabbering about.

"Lacey," Taylor said with frustration.

The girl didn't appear to have heard her because she kept gossiping about some girl that had gum stuck in her long blond hair. Really?

"Lacey," Taylor repeated louder this time.

The girl stopped talking.

"Thunder is a bundle of nerves." Not that Lacey seemed to have noticed. "Do you want to take a turn leading him? He's wearing me out." Taylor would gladly hand him over her new, chatterbox friend.

"Sure," Lacey said, stretching out her arm and taking hold of the lead rope. "Where do you think Kate is?"

Taylor had no idea where Kate was. "It's not like her to say she's meeting us and then not show up. She's reliable." For some reason Taylor felt she needed to defend Kate even if it looked like she changed her mind about the plan. "She's true to her word. I hope nothing happened."

"She didn't want to help with Thunder to begin with," Lacey said. Thunder snorted again. Lacey pulled his head down and forced him to relax. "Let's go, buddy."

The horse kept his head lowered and walked past the branch without so much as looking at it. Amazing. Taylor was usually a natural at getting horses to relax, but she'd used all her tricks and Thunder hadn't listened.

"You are doing a wonderful job with him," Taylor said, impressed.

The moonlight bathed Lacey's face with an angelic light and revealed her wide smile.

"As far as Kate goes," Taylor continued, "even if she changed her mind she would let me know." Again, Taylor was defending Kate. She hoped her best friend was safe.

"Maybe she isn't as brave as you think," Lacey said, attempting to plant doubt in Taylor's mind.

If Taylor hadn't known Kate as well as she did, she might be convinced to believe Lacey. "That's not her style," Taylor said. "I'm starting to get worried." Usually she was able to calm down her mind to the point where she had taught herself not to let emotions rule her decisions. Her mom said that came with maturity. Maybe it did, but right now she was worried about Kate.

"Call her cell phone," Lacey suggested.

Taylor knew that was a sticky subject with Kate. She didn't want to advertise the fact that Kate's parents refused to allow her to have her own cell phone. Actually, Taylor was unusual that way too. She chose not to have a cell phone because she didn't want people bothering her. She wasn't into social media, texting, or anything other than making occasional phone calls. Taylor had enough stress at home dealing with the twins, so when she went to the barn she wanted to focus on her horse. When she went to school, she wanted to focus on school. She realized she wasn't the norm, and she didn't care. But Kate cared.

On that note, Taylor didn't want to talk behind Kate's back because she knew how girls worked. Without a doubt, anything negative that Taylor said, or even remotely negative sounding, it would circulate around school. Friends were supposed to stick together. She decided to answer the comment without giving away Kate's personal details.

"Calling Kate is wonderful idea, but right now I want to concentrate on arriving safely at old man Brown's barn with Thunder." That wasn't so difficult. Taylor thought her answer was perfect, and it stopped Lacey's potentially harmful gossip about Kate.

Lacey continued to work magic with Thunder. He seemed more relaxed with her, and whenever he started to glance around, she'd get him to lower his head and walk by her side. It was obvious he liked her.

They turned off the main trail and onto the old wagon road. It was easy to miss but luckily the moon came out from behind a cloud and lit up the path. Taylor wondered if Kate had missed a path somewhere and ended up lost. Taylor was growing concerned about her friend.

When they approached old man Brown's house there was a light on in one of the first-floor windows. Why was he up at this hour? "Try to stay in the shadows." Taylor suggested to Lacey. "We don't want Mr. Brown to see us in the moonlight."

CHAPTER ELEVEN

Kate had no idea which way to start walking. She chose a random direction on the road and headed in that direction. Unfortunately, the cool breeze picked up. To fight off the cold, she zipped up her flimsy jacket. If only she'd planned ahead and brought warmer clothes. What if she didn't find her friends? She fought against the rising fear bubbling up in her, fought against the chill biting at her fingertips.

As she walked farther, she studied the houses, praying that at least one of them would look familiar. Of course, everything took on a different appearance at night, and the houses seemed bigger. Most of them had no lights on inside and there were no street lights in the neighborhood. She hoped everyone's dogs were inside and that she encountered no scary, wild animals that were hungry enough to eat a lightweight girl. Swallowing the lump in her throat, she fought back tears.

The comfort of her safe bed begged her to

return home and climb in it. Her parents would never know she ventured out, and she could wake up and eat breakfast as normal. All would be good, except for one thing. She was loyal to the bone and depending on where the road led, if she was anywhere near old man Brown's house, she wanted to find her friends.

The road turned out to be long and windy. Several streets in their neighborhood were similar, so it did next to nothing to help her figure out where she was. That was until the road took a sharp turn and aimed downhill. There on the left side was a daunting house with one light on downstairs on the side of the house. The light lit up a grass road that ran along the property. Kate recognized it immediately. She was at old man Brown's house, and the grass road was the wagon road.

Kate tried to swallow the lump that remained in her throat. She knew where her friends were, and if she was able to safely pass by Mr. Brown's house without him seeing her, then she'd soon join them.

A man walked in front of the illuminated window. He was pacing back and forth, as if he were talking on the phone. With the moonlight so bright, she had no idea how was she going to pass by the window without being seen.

Mr. Brown stopped and leaned against the glass, looking out into the pasture. Kate could see dark figures grazing in the field. One of the horses had his head up and was looking her way. Horses were so aware of their environment. As long as Kate didn't spook the herd and make them run, they wouldn't attract his attention. Mr. Brown turned his back to her, but when one of the horses called out into the night, he turned his head in their direction. Was the horse calling out to Kate, or maybe Thunder?

She hadn't thought about that piece of the plan. The horses would be curious as to who the new horse was in the old barn. Taylor and Lacey had to walk Thunder by a corner of their pasture, so the horses knew he was there. They'd want to sniff him, to see him, to know who he was, possibly creating a ruckus. She hoped they wouldn't run around the pasture tomorrow in the daylight, where Mr. Brown would for sure notice.

Kate hid in the shadows until she reached a brightly lit section of the road with no shadows. It happened to be right in front of where Mr. Brown stood at the window, and there was no way of passing by without being seen. She waited patiently at the edge of the shadow. How was she going to reach her friends?

She waited a few moments, and to her delight, a cloud passed in front of the moon. The entire road turned into one big shadow. Kate started running for the other side, but the risk was when the moon came back out she had no idea what part of the road would be moonlit and what part shadowed. She ran as fast as she could, tripping once in a hole, but she didn't allow that to stop her. She wasn't about to be caught.

The moonlight started to creep back out. Kate ran under a tree and prayed she'd be fully shadowed. The night grew brighter and thankfully she was standing in the perfect spot to stay hidden. She glanced up at the window and gasped. From this angle she saw Mr. Brown clearly. He seemed to be staring right at her.

Breathe, she commanded silently. She reminded herself that there was no way he could see her. Or could he? She gasped again.

She remained frozen for the longest time. If only he left the window, maybe sat down on the sofa to finish his phone conversation, she'd be able to continue on her way. She hoped by the time she reached Taylor and Lacey that they'd still be at the barn with Thunder. Otherwise, all this effort would be wasted. She decided not to come back this way along the road, it was too big of a risk. If she started from the old barn, already on the wagon trail, she wondered if finding the way home would be easier.

Old man Brown remained at the window chatting on the phone. He looked angry, nodding his head and waving his right hand. With his obvious bad mood, she didn't want to tangle with him tonight if he caught her. She had a strong urge to escape. But how? She was growing impatient and wanted to reach her friends as soon as possible.

Mr. Brown turned his head to look the other way. Kate decided to make a run for it, keeping to the shadows as much as possible. She'd be long gone if he came outside looking for her.

Her heart pounded so hard she heard the thumping in her ears. She kept running, though, and didn't dare look back. At the fork in the road, she turned right onto the trail and ran down the wooded path to the old barn. There was no one there! It was silent.

The window of Thunder's stall was shut and the barn was dark. Kate entered the back of the barn, but it was eerily quiet … and dark.

Wasn't Thunder here yet? Certainly he wouldn't be that quiet if he were alone in the barn. He'd be curious as to who arrived. She'd hear him moving around. If they weren't here yet, where were they?

Kate remembered the flashlight in the tack room. She opened the door, a loud creak filling the quiet. The tack room was unbelievably dark except for one small window high up on the back wall. Kate fumbled around to find the flashlight on the shelf where they'd left it. It wasn't there.

Confused about what to do next, Kate stood there and listened. She heard the faintest movement coming from the barn aisle. Was it Mr. Brown? Had he seen her?

The familiar lump returned to Kate's throat. There was no swallowing it no matter how hard she tried.

She peeked around the doorframe of the tack room and glanced in the direction of Thunder's stall. Her eyes were adjusting to the darkness and she swore she saw movement coming from his stall. Scared, she took a step out into the aisle. The dust must be stirred up still because she sneezed loudly. If Mr. Brown was in there, no doubt, he'd hear that sneeze.

The movement from the stall stilled. Kate crept closer and peered inside. Something dark and large moved toward her and she yelped. Thunder's breath blew on the side of her face.

"Oh, Thunder!" Kate said. "It's only you." She stuck her hand in between the stall bars and petted his nose. "You scared the heck out of me."

Another movement from a dark corner of the stall startled her again.

"Kate," someone whispered.

"Taylor?" Kate asked.

"Yes. Thank God it's you!" Taylor stood up, followed by more movement next to her. Lacey!

"You scared us to death," Taylor said, sounding short of breath. "We thought you were old man Brown."

"Me too," Kate admitted. "I thought you both

already left. I saw old man Brown standing in his window. I stood still for a while, but I finally ran down the road. I thought he followed me here."

Taylor and Lacey dusted off their jeans while Kate opened the stall door to give Thunder a proper greeting.

"Hey, boy. How do you like your new stall?" Kate asked, running her hand down the side of his neck.

He tossed his head as if he were say he loved it. She swore horses understood the English language.

"What happened to you?" Lacey asked. "We were getting worried."

Kate inhaled a deep breath of horse to calm her nerves. There was nothing like horse therapy. "I got lost in the woods. I couldn't find the wagon road in the moonlight and I ended up on some street. I followed it and realized I was by old man Brown's house." She inhaled another breath to fill her lungs with sweet horse smell. It always calmed her down. "Mr. Brown was standing in the window. I managed to work my way down the wagon road without him noticing me. At least I hope he didn't see me," she added.

"We saw his light on," Lacey said. "I thought you changed your mind about tonight."

Kate figured that was what Lacey thought.

"That's because you don't know her well enough yet," Taylor said, defending Kate. "If she says she's going to do something, she does it."

Thank you, Taylor. She was grateful her friend had her back. Maybe the word at school now wouldn't get around that Kate was a baby, because she wasn't. She'd proven it tonight. Even though she didn't necessarily care for Lacey, it was smart to stay on her good side.

CHAPTER TWELVE

That night, a night she'd never forget, Kate made it back to the safety of her bed. The trail had been difficult to see, even with Taylor's keen sense of sight, but the girls picked their way through. No wonder why she'd gotten lost before. She hoped her friends found their way home too after they had walked Kate to her house.

Her eyes grew heavy and before she knew it, the sun peeked through the blinds of the window in her room as if the warm light wanted to wake up Kate in the coziest way possible. Kate loved Sunday mornings at her house. The smell of pancakes wafted up the steps and entered her room. She crawled from bed, still dressed from the night before, and slipped her feet into the sneakers that she was supposed to keep in the basket by the front door. She had to meet her friends at the old barn to feed Thunder before church, that was, if she was able to convince her mother to allow her to leave.

At the last minute Kate decided it was best to change out of her dirty clothes. The last thing she wanted was for her mother to notice the dirty jeans and ask questions. Kate kicked her shoes back off, stripped her clothes onto the floor, and then as an afterthought she picked them up to stack atop the heaping pile in the hamper basket. Time was short before they left for church. She hurried and changed into clean barn clothes before making her way downstairs to the kitchen.

Her mother looked up after flipping a pancake. "Good morning, sweetheart."

To Kate's surprise, a rush of guilt flooded her. Never before had she sneaked out of the house at night, deceiving her parents, taking a risk of compromising their trust. If Kate knew how awful she'd feel, she wouldn't have agreed to the plan to begin with. The shame was almost too much. The humor in all this? They were going to church this morning, a contradiction to last night's adventure and to the Christian lifestyle her parents taught. Somehow she had to keep a straight face. Lying, or in this case keeping secrets, wasn't her usual behavior or something she even respected.

"Good morning," her mother repeated. "How are you feeling? Your mind seems a million miles away."

Kate's mom read her moods easily and,

unfortunately, today was no exception. "I'm fine. I didn't sleep well." That was the truth.

Her mother poured a cup of steaming, awesome-smelling coffee. Too bad coffee didn't taste as good as it smelled. Kate tried it once and it had tasted like watery mud.

"I woke up in the middle of the night and checked on you."

Kate inhaled a jagged breath. She fought down rising panic. Did her mother know she left the house last night?

Even though she had shoved two pillows under her comforter, a make-shift effort to make her bed look as though she slept in it, maybe her mother had still noticed she was missing. What time had she checked on her?

Kate inhaled slow, long breaths, attempting the breathing exercises her trainer had taught her. Layne swore by the technique to help Kate relax over jumps to chase away anxiety. The method usually worked well. The idea was to prevent her from holding her breath, creating more tension and anxiety in both Kate and Razor. The true test was to see if the exercises worked well in different situations such as the current one.

To her surprise, Kate's mind started to clear enough to allow her to stay calm. If she played it cool, Kate reminded herself, one way or another her mother would reveal the information without Kate having to ask.

"You were sleeping like a bear hibernating."

A gush of air released from Kate's lungs. She had been holding her breath again without realizing. Her mother's comment was the best news she had heard all week. Apparently, Kate was in bed when her mother tucked her in.

"I covered you up. You didn't move." Her mother flipped the pancakes, loaded with a generous amount of chocolate chips scattered across the top layer, and then took a slow sip of coffee from the mug Kate bought her last Christmas. Guilt, and more guilt. She had not predicted she'd be eaten up by shame.

"I have to admit, though," Kate's mom continued, "I was surprised to see you sleeping in your clothes."

Kate gulped. She'd changed clothes this morning for nothing, even brushed the dirt off the sheets. The idea of no one noticing seemed a stupid thought now.

Her mother stared at her. "Aren't you speaking this morning?"

Kate hadn't realized she'd remained quiet, lost in her own thoughts. "Sorry," she said. "Guess I'm still waking up." Another truth. See, she wasn't all bad. She was capable of some honesty.

"We're going to church at ten this morning."

Go figure that her mom mentioned church right

at the moment Kate's guilt was starting to ease.

"Why so early?" Kate whined. She didn't mean to be ungrateful but her friends were waiting at old man Brown's barn. She also wanted to see firsthand that Thunder was adjusting well to his new environment. If she were late again, or worse yet, if she didn't show up, her friends would never forgive her.

Her mother grew silent. That was more unnerving than if she had raised her voice. Did she know Kate was up to something? She risked a glance at her mother. Sure thing. Her eyebrows were lifted high in question.

"Be ready by 9:30," her mom said in a serious tone meant to stop Kate from complaining further.

Kate glanced at the clock. If she hurried, she'd have enough time to make it to old man Brown's barn to feed Thunder, check on him, and then return home to change clothes before church. The timing was tight. She needed to get moving. Kate grabbed an apple from the fruit bowl and headed for the door.

"Where are you going?"

How was she supposed to answer without lying? Kate despised the way the secret dug its claws into her soul, making her act in ways she didn't recognize. She prided herself on being honest, on being truthful in a way people understood without becoming defensive. Her father always said it was one of her best traits.

"I'm meeting the Horse Club at the barn for about a half hour." Kate slipped into the old barn shoes sitting by the back door. "I'll be ready for church on time," she called back. "Promise." Her mother liked communication, so that ought to do the trick.

Her mother narrowed her eyes instead. "If you aren't back here by 9:00, I'll be at the barn to pick you up. You'll have to go to church in your barn clothes."

Kate swallowed hard. If that were the case, her mother would realize that she wasn't at the usual barn, and that Thunder was missing. "No need to do that," Kate said, pulling the backdoor open. "I'll be here." She'd make a point to be early.

"Fine," her mother said, her voice doubtful.

Kate scurried out the door before her mother changed her mind. It was amazing how much easier the trail was to follow in the daylight, but she had to be more careful this morning because she was in clear sight. There were no dark shadows to hide in like last night, and no shade this early. She prayed old man Brown wasn't staring out his window, or drinking coffee on his back deck.

When she reached the backside of the old man's house, the horses in the pasture were gone. Kate thought she heard someone in his barn, perhaps feeding them. If that was the case, there was a chance of Kate not only being seen, but being heard too. She walked quietly, hoping when Thunder spotted her that he wouldn't neigh. If he did, whomever was in the barn would hear him.

She hurried her steps to get out of eyesight, not to mention she was on limited time.

Within minutes the weathered barn was in view. Thunder's stall window was shut tight, so that helped prevent him from seeing her. All seemed quiet, almost too quiet.

She approached the barn and rolled the wooden door open enough to slip in. Her eyes took a moment to adjust to the dim lighting but she made out an object in the nearest stall. Thunder stood at the stall door, curious about the visitor and new routine. She opened the feed room and scooped up the usual amount of pellets Layne had been feeding him. A low nicker escaped deep from Thunder's throat.

Kate smiled as she brought the feed to him and dropped it from the scoop into his clean corner feeder. It had taken forever to scrub off the years of grime from the bucket. Her hard work gave her a sense of accomplishment and satisfaction. She went back into the feed room, placed the scoop back into the bin, making sure to tighten the latch, and chose two large flakes of hay. When she turned around, she yelped. There, standing in the doorway, was Taylor and Lacey. Kate hadn't heard them enter the barn.

"Sorry to scare you," Taylor said. She leaned a shoulder against the doorframe. She was dressed in casual jeans, a lightweight flannel shirt, and had her bushy hair pulled back in a ponytail, a cute look for her. "I would have gotten here earlier but I had to help make breakfast for the twins."

"And I woke up late," Lacey added. She stood behind Taylor, looking over her shoulder, dressed like a model with designer jeans, a fitted, lightweight sweater, and a thin, colorful scarf.

Why was she dressed up to work in a dusty barn? Lacey wasn't a church person, so Kate ruled that out.

She decided to ask. "You look fancy. What's the occasion?"

Lacey blushed.

Her silence made Kate's belly knot. "Well?

"I'm meeting a friend at the mall." Lacey slid a strand of long hair behind her ear.

A friend? Kate didn't like the sound of that. "A guy?" Kate pressed, staring directly into the other girl's eyes.

Lacey squirmed.

"Name?" Not that it was Kate's business, but her gut instinct told her she needed to know.

Lacey turned her head away.

Kate didn't let up. If the sinking, sick feeling in her belly meant what she thought then she wanted to hear the honest truth from Lacey's mouth.

With her head still turned, Lacey mumbled, "Sam."

Lacey might as well have delivered a punch to Kate's belly, forcing out what little breath remained.

Taylor exhaled a low whistle.

Kate fought the urge to yell at Lacey, to yank the hair out of the girl's head. Instead, she took a long, deep breath. It was a great time to practice Layne's breathing technique, the second time this morning. When Kate's head cleared the tiniest bit, she reasoned that if Sam wanted to date the fake Lacey, then let him. Kate would have a hard cry tonight when she was alone in bed, but not now, not in front of the other girls.

"It's not what you think." Lacey shifted from one leg to another, and then back again.

Was Lacey nervous?

"Really? How so?" Kate fought to keep calm. She held on tighter to the flakes of hay she carried to avoid dropping them.

Lacey walked off but not before she said the all-too familiar phrase that, in Kate's opinion, guilty people used as an excuse. "We're just friends."

Not willing to let the conversation drop, Kate followed Lacey into the aisle and stopped in front of Thunder's stall, all the while holding onto the two flakes of hay. "Just friends. Right. And my mother is male." Kate tried to hide any expression from showing on her face but failed miserably. Her eyebrows were pulled into such a tight scowl her face hurt. She fought the urge to growl.

Taylor burst out laughing, not at the situation but from Kate's comparison to her mother being male. They knew each other's humor well enough to understand the sarcastic meaning behind Kate's words.

Lacey glanced back with a puzzled look on her face. "You're getting worked up over nothing." She poked her arm through the bars of the stall door to rub Thunder's face. He had finished eating his feed and was waiting for Kate to give him hay. When Kate approached the stall, Thunder poked his nose up to the bar and flapped his lips, trying to get a nibble of a stray hay.

"If you haven't noticed," Kate said with confidence, "I'm not worked up at all. Your slimy behavior doesn't surprise me."

Lacey's mouth dropped open. "What's that supposed to mean?"

"Take it however you want." Kate slid through the narrow opening after Taylor rolled the heavy stall door open. The low rumble of a nicker sounded from Thunder's throat as he followed Kate. She shoved the hay into the corner bin until it fit neatly to minimize spillage. "Here you go, sweet boy." He munched happily in answer.

Kate played with his mane, running her hands through thick strands as she took her time to gather her complicated emotions, despite her calm, outward appearance. As well as Layne's breathing techniques, Kate's father taught her to remain calm when stressed. He was always in control of his emotions and never raised his voice. Her mother said it had to do with inner peace, or something like that. Kate was trying to do well in this situation but wished she could achieve that mysterious peace when riding Razor. She hated being scared of jumping, trail riding, or whatever else. The fear of riding was a never-ending battle.

"Like I said, you have nothing to worry about," Lacey said, peering in from outside the stall.

Kate inhaled three long breaths before responding. "I'm not worried at all." She stepped away from Thunder and strode toward the open door. "In fact, I have a great sense of right and wrong. If you want to hang out with someone else's boyfriend, that says a lot about you." Kate, feeling empowered, snapped the stall door into place.

Taylor remained quiet, her mouth dropped open.

"Well, saying it that way is rather rude." Lacey hadn't moved away from the safe little spot she'd made for herself outside the stall by the corner feeder.

"Rude or not, it's the truth." Kate walked away.

She glanced at her watch. She had just enough time to return home to dress for church. "See you this evening at feeding time. I have somewhere to be." With that, she left the barn. Kate didn't glance back, but if she had, she was sure she'd see two shocked faces. Proud of herself, she strode along the trail past old man Brown's house without so much as a glance in his direction.

As she sat in church, though, she had trouble forgetting the whirlwind of events that happened over the past few days. She was growing up, or maturing as her mother would say, but the lies and secrets were eating her up inside. The pastor stood at the front of the church preaching about forgiveness of sins. In silence she prayed for forgiveness but she didn't feel better. Her trusting parents sat there, absorbing his message, as guilt flooded Kate. Shame for past sins and future ones filled her. She'd need all the forgiveness possible.

CHAPTER THIRTEEN

When Kate's mom dropped her off at the barn, Layne greeted them in the parking lot. Kate wanted to disappear under the seat in front of her.

"We seem to have a problem," Layne said into the open window of the car. Her voice was a combination of anger and anxiety.

"What's wrong?" Kate's mom was calm, at least until she heard the news about Thunder.

"We had a runaway horse staying with us." Layne looked around Kate's mom and spotted Kate in the backseat, her piercing eyes drilling into Kate's.

Kate fought the urge to sink in her seat. Her right arm started to tingle, then she realized she was pushing hard against the car door, wanting to escape. She straightened against the back of the seat and sat up straight.

"The girls showed a lot of interest in the

horse." Layne continued to stare at Kate as if trying to unnerve her so she'd admit to hiding the horse. "The horse disappeared last night from his stall."

The words hung in the air. Kate's mom didn't respond.

"I think the girls are involved," Layne said without blinking.

Kate's mom sat there, taking a moment to absorb the information. "I'm sorry, I don't understand."

"I threatened to send Thunder to a horse rescue," Layne said. She was no longer staring at Kate but engaging in eye contact with her mother. "The girls are upset with me. The night before the horse was to leave, he disappeared."

Silence.

Kate knew her mom was trying to figure out Kate's involvement in the mess. At first she'd think Kate was innocent, then she'd add up all the strange behavior lately, such as sleeping with her dirty clothes on, and running out early Sunday morning to meet her friends at the barn before church.

Her mother slowly turned her head toward Kate, who sat without moving.

"Kate?"

Kate didn't dare answer.

Her mother raised her eyebrows. "Are you involved in Thunder's disappearance?"

How to answer? Kate hadn't led him from one

barn to the other because she had been late. But she knew where he was, and yes, she was involved in cleaning up the old barn and taking care of Thunder. Her mind screamed out the word "Yes!" but her lips remained glued together. She had to come clean to be free from the guilt. But her friends were counting on her.

"I'm going to understand your silence as guilty." Her mother's eyebrows were no longer arched but scrunched into a straight line with a deep set of wrinkles between them, the look of brewing anger.

Layne's eyebrows took on a similar expression. With nowhere to run or hide, Kate slid downward in the seat, making a safe nest between the leather seat and the door.

Another car pulled up. Taylor! Let the adults harass her for a moment.

And then Lacey's car pulled into a parking spot. Never had Kate thought she'd find relief in seeing that traitor.

Layne whirled around on the heels of her tall boots and approached Taylor's car first. Her hands waved back and forth as she talked. Lacey's mom rolled down her window, heard part of the discussion, and stepped from their car. The engine was still running as if the woman needed a get-away car in case the conversation grew heated.

Kate's mom kept the car window down and the

discussion spilled into the car like smoke invading precious, clean air.

"The stall door was left open, his halter gone." Layne's hands were still swinging around.

Lacey's mom stuck her head out of her window. "Maybe someone stole him."

Layne's arm froze in the air for a moment before they started swinging around again. "Who would steal him?"

"Maybe his owner found him and led him home." Kate's mom was reasonable and defending the girls. More guilt.

From Kate's limited view from the tight corner she'd cuddled into against the seat, she noticed the other girls didn't move either. Layne shot her hands in the air as though giving up. At least for now.

Layne stormed off and disappeared into the barn, probably heading to her office to burn off frustration. Reluctantly, the girls climbed from their cars, but as Kate shut the car door, her mom said, "Kate, I hope you had nothing to do with the disappearance of that horse. I'm sure you know better."

Kate's throat constricted and no words left her mouth. She tried to say something, but really, what was there to say? Try the truth, her logical mind reasoned. Don't you dare, her emotional mind answered. The adults would be watching closely.

She left the car behind, not responding to her

mother, not glancing back. Dishonesty was a horrible character flaw. Kate wished she could spin back time to make different choices. Too bad that was impossible.

Razor greeted her at the stall door. A low rumble sounded from his throat.

"I'm happy to see you too." Kate lifted the halter off the brass hook, then slid the stall door open. He nuzzled her with affection. She pulled a treat from the zipped pocket of her riding pants and rewarded him. "We're going to have another star ride today. Aren't we?"

He nodded as if he understood.

They had extra pressure to perform well today because Layne would be on guard, looking for any reason to scold them.

Kate tacked up fast, in a hurry to burn off the stress from the earlier confrontation in the parking lot. She didn't wait for Taylor, mounted Razor, and headed up to the riding arena alone. Taylor and Layne weren't there yet, but Lacey was, unfortunately.

Ignoring the other girl, Kate warmed up Razor in the arena while she waited for the others to arrive. She wished she were anywhere but here. She'd rather avoid Layne, and Lacey reminded Kate of Sam. Not that Kate had a choice; her mother insisted she ride.

"You have a show coming up and need to

practice," her mother reasoned.

Her mom was right, but wisdom didn't help the situation. Every time Kate thought about Lacey and Sam at the mall together, Kate clenched her teeth. She didn't want to ride today. Period.

Lacey cut the arena in half and caught up to Kate.

"We're just friends." Lacey nudged harder to keep up with Razor and to speed up Spot, a new schooling horse who was slower than slow. Razor's natural pace was twice as fast as Spot's.

Determined not to let Lacey know how bothered she was by the whole "Sam thing," she shrugged her shoulders. "Whatever. I'm glad you had fun." Another lie.

Lacey tossed back her head and smiled. The rim of her helmet shaded her face but Kate saw the twinkle in her eye. No way did she have innocent feelings for Sam.

"We walked around the mall, shared one of those big pretzels and a Coke, and decided to watch a movie." Lacey jabbered on, apparently clueless of the tension running through Kate's body. "There was this new movie that I was dying to see."

A pain, no, a knife carving out Kate's stomach made her flinch. The last thing she wanted to hear about was how Lacey and Sam shared a snack at a movie.

"Sounds like a date to me." Kate nudged Razor

into a trot and left Lacey and Spot behind.

"You're jealous," Lacey called after her.

And you're a poor excuse for a human being! Kate started the now-familiar breathing techniques, instead of speaking her mind. *Breathe.* Razor tossed his head, trotting faster, picking up on Kate's tension in her body.

She wasn't supposed to hate people. Right now Kate despised Lacey.

Kate warmed up at the trot and then cued Razor to canter.

"If you ride like that in the next horse show, you'll kick some butt." Layne opened the arena gate and entered through the opening with Taylor and her horse, Frankie, behind her.

Maybe anger was the answer to placing better in horse shows. Kate needed to compete against her enemy, Lacey, so her focus wasn't on the fear of jumping but instead on how much she despised the other girl. Interesting thought, one Kate needed to explore. The next horse show, a first for Kate with Razor, was around the corner and she planned to enter. Chances were, Kate would ride against Lacey.

"Taylor, go ahead and warm up." Layne walked into the center of the arena to increase the height of one of the fences.

Kate gulped at the size of the oxer. The anger toward Lacey disappeared and the familiar fear of jumping returned. So much for the thought of anger replacing fear. It gripped its claws deep inside her. The confusing thing was she loved jumping, after the fact, after the lesson was over when she was safe.

Layne instructed them to jump a small crossrail to continue their warm up. Razor tripped over it, barely making an effort. Kate wasn't fooled by his lazy side because she knew he'd jump the large oxer with enthusiasm.

The lesson went well, with Kate aware of Lacey's watchful stare. Too bad the traitor had to ride with them. If Kate made an error, Lacey would gossip at school, making sure to fill Sam in on how awful Kate rode. No pressure. Right. She needed to ride her best. In fact, so far the ride was awesome, until it came time to jump the oxer.

"Kate, it's your turn." Layne stood there expecting her to jump without argument.

Breathe. All the breathing techniques in the world wouldn't help with the anxiety dancing in her belly.

"You can do it," Lacey said.

Lacey was encouraging her?

Confused, Kate nudged Razor into a canter. The world disappeared as she focused on the pace of Razor's stride, figuring out their take-off spot, and breathing, of course. As they approached the oxer her belly knotted into a cramping clump of mess. Breathe. Razor locked his gaze on the oxer as if she asked him to perform the most important job ever. He remained calm, in control of himself. They left the ground with ease, floating through the air, and landed smoothly. No big deal. Until Layne asked her to jump it again.

Kate continued to canter around the arena, turning her head to watch for the jump. Razor was loving this. He lifted his head, ears trained on the oxer, and flew over it as if he wanted to fly. He deserved someone who showed at a higher level. Kate wasn't that person.

"Whoop!" Layne yelled. "You go, girl! Stop on that one and cool him out. You are finished."

What a relief.

It was Taylor's turn. Frankie had a smaller, faster stride. They fit together well, rode like a team. Taylor saw her take-off spot and moved forward without hesitation. She cleared the oxer with accuracy and bravery, but in comparison, Kate had grace and excellent form. In a horse show the judge would have a hard time choosing which to place higher.

Up next, Lacey cued Spot to canter but had a hard time keeping him moving. She missed her takeoff spot and, because her pace was off, crashed through the oxer, knocking the back pole onto the ground. Lacey landed on his neck with her feet searching for both stirrups.

Kate gasped. Even though she despised Lacey most of the time, she wanted her to be safe. *Stay on, don't let go.*

Spot realized Lacey was in trouble and slowed to a walk. What a good boy. She was able to slide down his neck, back into the saddle.

"What a ride," Layne called out. "Next time keep your heels down, eyes up, and move him forward like you mean business."

Shaken, Lacey nodded in answer.

Kate had been worried about Lacey judging her riding, but never did it occur to her that Lacey wasn't perfect. Was Lacey concerned about Kate blabbing at school about almost falling off? Doubtful. Then why did Kate care so much about what Lacey thought?

CHAPTER FOURTEEN

"Hold onto him!" Lacey yelled, seemingly tense as a little kid on the first day of school.

"I am." Kate held onto Thunder's reins as he trotted in place. "It's a bad idea to ride him. We don't know if he's ever had someone on his back before."

"That's why we're going to lunge him first." Taylor poked the end of the lunge line through one side of Thunder's bit, over his ears, and hooked it onto the other side.

The small clearing was well hidden from old man Brown's house, but not from someone riding on the nature trail. Most people didn't venture down the smaller trail, but if they wanted a quick cool down for their horse, this was the path they usually chose. Kate tried not to think about someone showing up unannounced.

Thunder continued to dance around. "Let me try," Taylor said, reaching for the lunge line. Kate handed it over to her, glad to be free of the responsibility. They had smuggled a bridle, lunge line and whip from the big barn. They planned to ride Thunder bareback because the old saddle they found in the tack room was filthy. They also didn't have a saddle pad or a girth. Besides, that was too much to carry from the barn without someone noticing. Nope, bareback was the plan, a crazy plan at best.

It was obvious Thunder knew what he was doing because he lunged on a circle with ease. He tossed his head and bucked a few times, but overall, he was calm.

"This should be a breeze," Lacey said. "I told you he's been ridden before. I bet he was a show horse."

"Just because he can lunge doesn't mean he's been ridden." Kate watched from the edge of the field where it was safe. Why was she the only one with common sense? The thought of riding a horse they knew nothing about was plain stupid. And asking for trouble.

"If we're going to keep him, he needs to work." Taylor was always so practical even if her bravery caused her to take unnecessary chances. "We're taking a big risk by hiding him. He's costing us a lot of money, so he needs to earn his keep." Taylor finished lunging him in circles. He did seem more relaxed now.

"Who plans to ride him?" Kate was smart

enough not to volunteer.

"I will." Lacey stood. She brushed off dirt from her riding pants from sitting on the dirt path that wound its way past the field.

Lacey was as brave as Taylor. Kate wasn't sure that was smart, but it pointed out Kate's weaknesses once again. Her father always told her fear wasn't a fault, that it was her mind's way of instructing her how to remain safe. He said everyone had fear to some degree. Fear can be good as long as it didn't keep you from growing as a person. Not offering to ride Thunder fell under the category of keeping herself safe.

Taylor led him to the center of the field. Thunder had his head down, relaxed, awaiting their next request. Little did he know that they planned for Lacey to sit on his back. If all went well, she'd ride him around the field without difficulty.

Lacey pointed at a stump. "I'll use that to climb on him." Mounting was the most crucial part of riding. Lacey would be most vulnerable with her leg resting over the horse's back until she sat on him. If anything went wrong, she could be hurt seriously.

Taylor led him to the stump and handed him over to Lacey. She stepped up onto the makeshift mounting block, took a deep breath, and gathered the reins in her left hand. Only because Kate was the queen of the breathing technique did she notice Lacey inhale three long breaths and let each of them out slowly. She was nervous, as well she should be.

"Be careful," Kate warned. For the second time she found herself concerned about Lacey's safety despite her dislike for the girl.

Lacey glanced back, her face softening. "I will."

Taylor stood in front of Thunder to keep him from moving forward. Kate positioned herself on his right side to prevent him from scooting sideways, and to assist Lacey if needed.

"Rub his side with your hand first." Taylor had trained young horses before, so she knew what she was talking about. "Lean on him with your arms, one at a time. If that goes well, reach over him and rub his other side."

Taylor was more qualified than Lacey and would be a better choice to ride him for the first time, but Kate wasn't going to voice her concern. One thing was for sure, Lacey needed to stay safe.

No one knew where they were. They were alone in the woods. What if an emergency happened?

"If his head stays low and relaxed," Taylor instructed, "lean your body against his. Put more weight on him until you are lying across his back. Then slide your right leg across him."

Why did they choose to do this bareback? Lacey had nothing to hold onto other than Thunder's mane.

Lacey followed what Taylor told her. Thankfully, Thunder seemed bored with the whole thing. She progressed to the point where she was lying across his back. He tried to take a step forward but Taylor stopped him. She gave him a rub on his forehead.

"Stop there," Taylor said. "Now that he's standing still, reward him by sliding off."

Lacey raised her eyebrows in silent argument.

"Trust me," Taylor said. "Go slowly. Patience."

Lacey didn't listen. She slid her right leg around Thunder's back. She leaned on his neck to take it easy but he thrust his head down. Lacey lost her balance, sliding down his neck, landing in a thud on the ground in front of his nose.

"I told you to back off!" Taylor gave Lacey her hand and helped her up. "Are you okay?"

Lacey's cheeks were bright red. "I'm fine."

Kate understood the girl's embarrassment. "Thunder wasn't upset with you on his back," Kate said. "He wanted grass to eat."

Lacey's gaze met Kate's. An understanding passed between them that the incident wouldn't be discussed again, here or at school. Lacey shifted her focus back to Thunder as she brushed off her riding pants. A long grass stain ran down the back of her leg. She climbed back up on the stump ready to repeat the process.

This time, when she brought her leg around his

back and sat upright on him, he didn't move. He stood quietly with his head low and relaxed.

"Good boy," Taylor said. She rubbed his forehead as a reward.

"I'm telling you, he was a show horse." Lacey nudged Thunder forward, knocking Taylor out of the way.

A frown flashed across Taylor's face. Kate noticed the moment Taylor pushed the rude behavior aside and decided it wasn't worth allowing Lacey to make her upset. Kate needed to learn a lesson in just that, in not letting other people hurt her feelings and taking their actions personally. That was easier to say when she wasn't the one upset, though.

"Ride him at the walk around the field," Taylor instructed.

Lacey frowned from being told what to do, but she listened. She'd likely had enough embarrassment for the day. Thunder behaved well as she walked him in a small circle. The horse was flat out gorgeous. Lacey might have guessed right that he was a show horse. It wasn't difficult to imagine him sailing over fences with style.

He broke into a trot, floating across the ground with ease. What an awesome mover. He'd win any flat class, which was walk, trot, canter without jumping.

Lacey sat the trot as if he were barely moving.

When she asked him to canter, her bottom stayed glued to his back. While riding him, her skill level elevated to a much higher level. The two of them fit together like a dream.

A squirrel darted from a nearby brush pile. Thunder scooted sideways, his eye's large with fear. He planted his feet, refusing to move forward in the direction of the squirrel. His loud snort rang out in the quiet afternoon air. The good news was that Lacey stayed on him.

"Come on, Thunder. You're fine." Lacey encouraged him to move his feet but he refused.

"Turn him in a circle." Taylor's voice was urgent.

Lacey tried to turn him in a controlled circle but he spun around and bolted, running like a racehorse through the small pasture. When he reached a large, fallen tree he stopped dead and turned. Lacey shot off him at what seemed the speed of a bullet. She hit the ground before Kate fully understood what happened.

"Lacey!" Taylor ran toward her.

Kate started to run too, but Thunder was racing around the pasture with his loose reins hooked on his ears. If he tossed his head, they'd fly over his ears and he'd likely step on them. Dangerous. Instead of running after Lacey, who was now sitting up in place, she went after Thunder. If he escaped and ran down the path, he'd likely return to the main barn where Layne was teaching lessons. That was, if old man Brown didn't spot him first.

"Thunder, whoa!" Kate tried to keep her voice calm. No chance.

He ran around the edge of the field, looking for an opening in the woods.

"Whoa, boy." Her voice sounded more controlled this time. She held out her hand as if she had a treat to offer him. He ran up to her but at the last moment darted around her. He found an opening in the trees and trotted through the thicket. Kate gasped as he ran toward a low-hanging branch in his path, but at the last minute, he ducked his head. He disappeared down the path.

Kate ran after him. When she reached the old barn he was standing still, tearing chunks of grass from the small area around his new barn. It was just short of a miracle that he hadn't returned to the big barn.

Kate tipped her head upward and said a prayer of thanks. She should have said a prayer for Lacey's protection before she'd climbed on Thunder.

Kate approached him slowly, holding out her hand. "Easy boy." He continued to munch as if he were starving, which meant his emotions were on full alert, but he continued to stand there eating. Kate stopped and gave him a chance to relax before she approached him.

He remained still. Grateful, Kate reached out

and took hold of the reins hooked behind his ears. Kate shook off the ugly image of him running with the reins swinging around, tempting a leg to get caught. She said another prayer of thanks.

"It's okay. You're fine." Kate ran her hand down his neck. He was sweaty from his workout and the additional run in the woods. "Let's walk so you can cool down before dinner." To his regret she lifted his head from the grass. He tried to resist but gave in quickly.

She prayed again for Lacey. If she wasn't okay, they'd all be in trouble.

CHAPTER FIFTEEN

Lacey walked with a limp at school the next day. When people asked why she ignored them, saying it was no big deal. The more she ignored them, the more attention she received.

Kate found it hard to keep the secret but they had no choice. She realized how lucky Lacey was that for the most part she was fine. Never once had she complained about deciding to ride Thunder. In fact, she planned to try again tonight.

It was risky riding without an adult knowing where they were. And the worst part? There was no way out of the entire situation without paying a huge price. Even if Kate wanted to come clean, a scary thought in itself, the rest of her friends wanted to keep the secret. That was peer pressure.

"I'll meet you after dinner tonight," Lacey said to Kate while waiting for a ride after school. Kate noticed several girls watching their interaction, probably wondering why Lacey was talking to someone unpopular as Kate was. Too bad. Kate shrugged off their stares.

She wanted to argue that she needed to spend time with Razor but Lacey didn't give her a chance. The other girl climbed in a car without waiting for an answer. That was fine. If Kate went straight home and finished her homework, grabbed a quick bite to eat, she'd have time to pull Razor's mane, clip him, and then meet the girls at old man Brown's barn. There was no question about it, maintaining two horses was proving difficult. There was a reason she leased Spirit to Candice. She didn't have time in her schedule for all this.

Her mother picked her up in front of the school. "Want to go shopping at the mall this afternoon?"

Of course Kate wanted to shop, but she had to decline. Thunder was fast taking over her life. "I can't, Mom. I have homework, and then I'm meeting my friends at the barn."

"That's all you do anymore," her mother said as she made a left turn out of school.

She was right, although Kate resisted admitting the truth. "I have a lot of responsibility. It's hard to keep up, but I'm managing."

"Everything okay?"

Was her mother suspicious, or simply being supportive?

"Sure." Kate didn't want to say anything more to avoid a lie. "I'd like to finish my homework, eat dinner quickly, and then head to the barn. Is that okay?"

Her mother turned onto their street. "Yes, honey. Your dad is working late so we're having leftovers. Eat them when you're ready."

At Taylor's house the entire family ate dinner together every night. Taylor complained about it, especially on nights she wanted to meet them at the barn, but Kate had to admit she was more than a little jealous. At least Taylor had a normal family. Her father returned from work at a decent time, her mother cooked and cared for the twins, and even though they didn't have a lot of money, they somehow managed to keep Taylor involved in horses. Horses were expensive, but that never stopped Taylor.

Taylor babysat, worked at her father's business doing light filing, and earned chore money. She helped pay for supplies for her horse and for shows. She didn't have to pay for all of it, but Kate gave her credit for helping.

In Kate's family, however, her father was a doctor. They had plenty of money, lived in a big fancy house, but it was vacant of warmth. Kate wanted to trade lives with Taylor. Money was nice, not that Kate was complaining, but she was lonely. Most of the time it was just Kate and her mother home. Kate loved her father, even thought he was a wise man, but she missed him.

"Well, enjoy your barn time." Her mother's words broke into Kate's deep thoughts so much that her mom's voice startled her. "My fondest memories of being a kid are that of my horse friends. I need to ride again."

Kate didn't want her mother at the barn. Even though she was lonely, she wanted a family life, not a barn mom.

Her mother pulled into the driveway. The yard man was riding the lawn mower around. Taylor's family mowed their own lawn.

Clueless to Kate's thoughts, her mom parked in the garage and tapped the remote to close the door. "I know, you don't want me following you around the barn, telling you what to do,"

Correct, but Kate remained silent.

"Mom, are you busy tomorrow night? We could go to the mall then." Her mother was right; they needed to spend time together. Kate was at the barn too much. Instead of complaining about her family life, or lack of, she needed to do something to fix the situation.

Her mother grinned. "It's a date."

Kate climbed from the car. Once she finished the small amount of homework she had, she'd be free to head to the barn before taking care of Thunder. Razor was her love. She was looking forward to giving him some tender loving care. He deserved it.

She whipped through a page of math and finished editing a paper due tomorrow. Then, after changing clothes, she went downstairs to reheat leftovers but her mother had beat her to it. There sitting on the table was Kate's dinner. The loving attention warmed her.

"I could go to the barn with you tonight," her mom suggested. "I promise not to critique your riding or offer advice."

Kate giggled. "That sounds fun, but not tonight if you don't mind. I'm meeting Taylor and another girl. We're hanging out."

"Is there a new girl in the Horse Club?"

That was a loaded question. "Not yet." Kate shoved a mouthful of leftover stir fry into her mouth and chewed. When she finished, she drank a gulp of green tea. Her mother was healthy conscious and insisted Kate eat right. "Lacey is her name. She wants to join the club but we haven't had time to vote her in."

"Is that the pretty girl I saw you talking to at school when I was in car line?"

Everyone always thought Lacey was pretty, even Sam. That was why she was popular.

"Yes, that's her." Kate shoved bite after bite into her mouth without talking. She was enjoying her mother sitting in the kitchen with her while she ate. To some people that wasn't a big deal, but to Kate, quality time was important. Even if they didn't talk much.

When she finished eating, Kate's mom offered to drive her to the barn. "That will save you time," she said. Was her mother lonely too? Did the quiet hours get to her as much as it did Kate? Interesting thought.

"Thanks." Kate slipped her barn shoes on at the door. Even though Kate wanted to spend time with her mom, she didn't want her to stay at the barn. If she did, it would be impossible to escape and run off to help Lacey ride Thunder.

CHAPTER SIXTEEN

Kate's mom didn't leave the barn when she dropped her off as promised. How was she supposed to meet her friends at old man Brown's barn?

She didn't want to be rude to her mother by suggesting she leave. Without complaint, Kate continued with her plan to pull Razor's mane and to clip him. His hair was fast growing out of control. If she saw a picture of just his head and neck she would think he was a fluffy pony.

Kate tugged out comb after comb full of mane. Before long a stack of loose hair piled up beside her on the ground. To Razor's credit, he remained still.

"He looks like a different horse already." Her mom removed the clippers from its case and plugged in the cord to an outlet by the crossties. Kate had to admit that it was cool at times that her mother shared the same interest.

She found herself enjoying their time together,

and for a short while she forgot about meeting up with Taylor and Lacey. When she remembered, however, anxiety darted through her.

"What's the matter?" Her mom always noticed her different moods. On some level it took Kate by surprise that she picked up on the slightest changes, but her mom was tuned in to the subtle differences in Kate.

"Oh, I promised I would drop you off," her mom said. She was taking the blame for Kate's mood shift. "I was enjoying myself so much I forgot."

Kate was having fun too. They rarely hung out together, talking and relaxing. What if she stayed at the barn instead of meeting her friends? Her mom was important, as well as her friends, but her mom was a priority. As their pastor often said in church, it was easy to be selfish. Life wasn't only about what Kate wanted. She had to factor in her mother's feelings too. Hadn't Kate silently complained earlier that she was lonely, that she wanted more time with her mother? She was being rewarded. Too bad the timing was off.

But the answer was simple. Kate would stay here with her mother and Razor. Her friends were expecting her, but to be honest, she was tired of the pressure. It was unfortunate she didn't have a cell phone, so she could text Taylor to let her know. She had to admit that life was easier without one, though. She could always run down to the old barn and tell them she wasn't coming, but that would take at least twenty-five minutes. Her mother would wonder where she had disappeared to. The only choice she had was to trust that her friends would understand.

They would have to understand. Period.

Her mother seemed to forget Kate's mood change and busied herself by running the clippers over Razor's nose, trimming off the long whiskers. When she finished his muzzle felt like velvet. From all the stimulation of the clippers, he relaxed his lower lip so it hung there. Kate loved to wiggle it back and forth. When he had had enough of her playing, he flapped his lips together, making a repetitive popping noise. Kate and her mom laughed.

Lacey appeared at her side. Kate raised her eyebrows in question as to why she wasn't at old man Brown's barn, either.

"Can I talk to you for a second?" Lacey asked.

To buy time for a moment as to not alert her mother, Kate ran her hand up Razor's nose and straightened his forelock as a display of affection. "Sure."

"Go ahead," her mom said, clippers still in hand. "I'll work on his bridle path while you're gone."

When they were out of earshot, Lacey said with

awe in her voice, "That's so cool your mom knows how to do horse stuff." She seemed almost jealous. "My mom stays far away from the barn. She'd rather do anything than come here."

Kate hadn't realized just how lucky she was until Lacey's comment. Kate had been afraid of what her friends might say about her mom hanging out at the barn, not realizing that they wished their parents took more of an interest in their hobby.

Lacey started talking fast. "I can't go to the barn tonight. I have a test tomorrow, a lot of homework, and it's my turn to make dinner. I think Taylor is babysitting."

Another blessing. Not only did her friends have other things to do, Kate was busy too.

Then a thought struck her. "Who will feed Lightning?" He deserved to have someone visit him for a while and brush him. He was alone in the barn with no buddies.

"I don't know. This is getting tough." Lacey sighed with frustration. "How are we going to keep up?"

"I'm having the same problem."

"Can you call Taylor and see if she can feed him later?" Lacey asked. "If she can't, I can zip by there and dump some food in his bucket, but I won't be able to stay."

Poor Thunder.

"I hope he isn't lonely," Kate said, knowing all

too well how that felt. Loneliness was the last thing she wanted for him.

"Me too." Lacey took a step toward the barn door. "Listen, I need to run. Let me know if Taylor can feed him." With that she hurried out the doorway, leaving Kate with the heavy burden of finding someone to care for Thunder.

How was she supposed to call Taylor? Kate's mom was standing there, not to mention she didn't have a cell phone. If she waited until she returned home to call, would that give Taylor enough time? The situation was fast turning into a mess.

Anxious, Kate returned to where her mother had finished clipping Razor's bridle path and was now working on his back leg. He stood still, taking a nap and not worrying about the clippers. He was worth the world to Kate, she realized.

Her mom glanced up to acknowledge Kate's return, and then refocused on the awesome job she was performing on his legs. Her mother knew how to clip a horse correctly. The sleek job made Kate want to enter a horse show. There was one next month. If she worked hard, they could be ready.

In the meantime, Kate needed to figure out what to do with Thunder. What if she blurted out the truth to her mother? What was the worst thing she'd say?

Kate could test the waters a bit to see how her mom reacted.

Her mom moved to Razor's front leg, the last little bit she had left to clip. Razor knew the routine and continued to nap.

The clipper buzzed lightly as her mom worked. They were the quietest clippers Kate ever owned. Usually they were so loud you weren't able to have a conversation.

"Mom, what would you do if something was bothering you but you couldn't tell anyone?" Kate's heart rate picked up. She tried to breath slowly to stay calm.

Her voice was easily heard over the hum because her mother glanced up.

"What's going on?"

Kate stared at Razor's open stall door. She didn't talk for a long moment. When she finally spoke, her voice sounded shaky. "That's the thing. I can't tell you because it involves other people."

"I see." Her mom studied her work and continued clipping without looking at Kate. It was possible she was avoiding adding pressure on Kate, as opposed to ignoring her. "And if you tell me, they'll get mad. Or in trouble," her mother said.

"Exactly."

"What does your mind tell you to do?"

Her mom was being so "cool." She understood complicated issues.

"To do the right thing and come clean."

Her mom stopped, clippers in hand, and studied

Kate. "Whatever is bothering you, I can tell it's something big. Sometimes you feel better when you tell someone what's troubling you."

She would feel lighter once she was out of the situation all together. Until then, she had to cope the best she knew how. Unfortunately she was afraid to come clean to her mother.

Kate turned away from staring at the stall door to watch her mom finish clipping Razor's front leg. "I'm not ready to say anything, but thanks for the conversation." It was reassuring to know Kate had someone to talk to if needed.

"Finished." Kate's mom ran a hand down Razor's leg to study her work. "He's show ready. Do you want to enter the next one?"

The real question? Was Kate ready to enter Razor in their first show? Her head nodded before the thought of competing Razor over jumps entered her mind.

"Make sure you're riding several times a week." Her mom rolled up the cord to the clippers and shoved the whole thing into the plastic box. It was always a tight fit. She had to move it around a few times before the lid snapped shut. "And Kate, just know that you can tell me anything. That doesn't mean there won't ever be a punishment involved, but I guarantee it will be less than if I found out on my own. I'd rather you be mature enough to tell me when something is wrong."

Kate swallowed hard. *Tell her.* But the words hid inside the lump in her throat. She wasn't ready to talk.

As soon as they walked in the front door of their house, Kate called Taylor.

"I can't feed him tonight, either," Taylor said. "One of the twins is sick and I have to babysit while my mother has a phone meeting."

Thunder needed feeding. He needed love, care, food, his stall cleaned. "How are we going to pull this off?" Kate asked. Her mother was readying herself for a trip to the mall. She'd talked Kate into shopping tonight.

"Can you run down there?" The healthy twin screamed in the background, pretending he was a police car. The wail of the siren echoed in the phone. "It won't take long."

Tell her mother. Be free of the stress.

"I can't. We're getting ready to leave."

"What can't you do?" Her mother walked into the room wearing makeup, her hair brushed smooth and gorgeous, and wearing dangly earrings. She was ready to leave.

How was Kate supposed to answer the question without lying? Hiding secrets was getting complicated. More guilt. "Taylor asked if I could help her with something before we go."

"Why don't I drive you over there?" Kate's mom asked.

Think fast. "It won't take long, Mom. I'll run down the street and be back before you know it."

With a scowl on her face, her mom agreed. She sighed and set down her purse as if she had to wait for hours. "Change clothes before you go so you're ready to leave."

Kate hung up the phone, gave her mom a kiss on the cheek, and promised to be home soon. She ran upstairs to change clothes into something casual enough for the barn but nice enough to wear shopping. She chose a new pair of jeans and a casual top. She trotted down the steps, slipped on the barn shoes waiting in the basket beside the back door, and left the house before her mother insisted on driving.

Kate ran halfway to the old barn but wasn't in decent shape enough to run the entire way. By the time she reached Thunder, she was out of breath and had a sharp pain in her side. She slid open the barn door, his greeting welcoming her.

"I know, buddy. You're in this dark barn." She opened the feed room, filled the scoop, and returned to his stall. "We can't ride you tonight but I promise, we'll get you out tomorrow." An idea popped into her mind. They hadn't had time to work on the overgrown lot that his stall door opened to, so she couldn't allow him out there yet, but she opened the top door so he had a view of the woods. "At least you can see outside. We'll work on your run so you can get out." The biggest problem with that was someone seeing him, but no one usually rode on the trail to the old barn because it led nowhere.

He munched on feed while she scooped shovels full of manure into a ratty muck bucket. "I'll dump that tomorrow, but at least your stall is clean." She dragged the bucket out of his stall and left it in the barn aisle. She went back into the feed room, grabbed two flakes of hay, and carried it back to his stall. She shoved it into the corner hay feeder as he finished the last bites of feed. "See you tomorrow." She patted his neck as an attempt to show him some love.

She returned home, again out of breath, and bumped into her mother when Kate opened the door.

"I thought you weren't going to be gone long?" Her mom studied Kate's clothes and inhaled a long breath. "You've been at the barn?"

Kate hadn't noticed a smudge of manure on her new jeans.

"What aren't you telling me?" Kate's mom sounded suspicious.

Just know that you can tell me anything. The punishment will be less than if I found out on my own.

The words haunted Kate's mind but she remained silent.

CHAPTER SEVENTEEN

Amazed at how well Lacey and Thunder fit together, Kate watched them closely. Lacey asked for the walk and Thunder listened. She asked for the trot, he trotted. No, he floated. They were a dream, partners, a team.

Kate was glad she would never have to compete against the two of them.

At some point Thunder had to return home to his owner. If he didn't, worst case scenario, someone would find out about him, or they'd have to confess to the adults. Either way, it was a matter of time before the secret exploded. Kate wasn't looking forward to that day.

"Push him forward," Taylor instructed Lacey.

Kate swore Lacey cringed from Taylor telling her what to do, but despite her resistance, she listened. She urged Thunder forward, and Kate's mouth dropped open in awe. He had a gorgeous trot with extended reach. Again, Kate thought he had to be a show horse. If not, she hoped he found his way into the show ring. Otherwise his amazing talent was wasted.

His canter flowed with perfect rhythm too. It was easy to imagine him sailing gently over a course of large jumps.

After a few minutes of a flawless canter, he stopped dead in his tracks. With his head held high, his ears perked, he stared down the trail. What did he hear?

A horse and rider appeared on the trail. Kate gasped. A horse named Bagel perked his ears upward toward them, and Sarah, the girl who told everyone she was *the* Sarah with an "H" on the end of her name, watched the Horse Club girls as she approached.

Sarah's eyes were wide with surprise. When she rode closer, she asked with her voice an octave too high, "What are you doing?"

Unbelievable. Their secret was out.

The girls didn't answer. They stood still, unable to speak.

Sarah's curious stare roamed to Thunder, who hadn't moved, either. Her eyes widened even more. "That's the missing horse," she whispered.

None of them recovered quickly enough to comment. Words were impossible to speak. What amazing timing. One moment Kate was admiring Thunder's beauty, the next, their enjoyable day ruined.

Sarah, with an "H," shook her head in disbelief. "And you're riding him," she hissed as she sat on her tall horse, staring down at them as if she were better than they were. Even with her delicate face shaded from her helmet, Sarah's narrowed eyes were obvious. "Wait until Layne hears about this. At the very least, she'll suspend you from entering the next horse show." If that happened, it would eliminate most of the competition for Sarah. Of course, she'd tell.

"Grow up," Taylor said with a firm voice.

Was Taylor ever intimidated by bullies, or anything for that matter?

Sarah smirked. "I hardly think you're in a position to be nasty."

The situation was growing interesting as Taylor and Sarah squared off.

"Slither out of here," Taylor ordered. "Don't look back."

Instead, Sarah dismounted. In her tight riding pants, showing off her perfect, rounded butt, stylish blue belt enclosing a crisp, tucked-in white designer shirt, she swayed over to Lacey and Thunder. Sarah's horse followed along like an obedient dog.

"What are you doing hanging out with these little girls, Lacey?" Sarah asked. "I thought you were friends with the popular girls. Why are you riding with the young Horsie Club kids?"

Kate frowned. It was one thing to cut them

down, but to poke fun at the Horse Club?

Lacey didn't reply. She sat still on Thunder as if to consider the answer.

"Are you a member of the Horse Club yet?" From the tone of Sarah's voice, it was obvious she didn't respect the Horse Club.

Kate's father, who was often right, would accuse Sarah of being jealous. Was that a possibility?

Lacey glanced between Kate and Taylor. "Yes, I'm a member of the club."

Kate wasn't sure when that happened. She hadn't voted her in, and she was sure Candice, the youngest member of the group hadn't, either.

"If you're a member, I want to belong to the club too." Sarah didn't ask. No, she forced her will on them.

Taylor shook her head. "Not a good idea."

Sarah ignored the comment, letting her horse graze on a clump of fresh green grass in the shade of a pine tree. The Horse Club members never allowed their horses to graze with the bridle on. It was one of the rules.

"Tell you what," Sarah said, not caring that her horse pushed his head into her personal space, chewing a wad of grass. The bit was already turning green. "You let me join the club, and I won't tell about stealing Thunder."

"We didn't *steal* Thunder." Taylor turned her

attention off Sarah. "Lacey, why don't you put Thunder away. I think we've had enough excitement for one evening."

Surprised that Lacey listened, Kate turned her head, trying to hide her shocked expression. How did Taylor have such authority? People, even Lacey, automatically listened to her. No one followed Kate's direction. What was the difference between the two of them? One word popped into Kate's mind. Confidence.

Kate needed to control her emotions more and project the appearance of cool, calm, and collected. That was difficult. Taylor naturally radiated confidence in most every situation without effort. How did a person reach that level? Was her friend fortunate enough to be born with confidence, or was it something she had to earn? Kate planned to solve the mystery someday.

Lacey disappeared with Thunder into the dark entryway of the barn. Kate had to admit, they made a cute team. Horse and rider fit each other well in size and personality.

"Like I said, let me join the Horse Club and I'll keep quiet."

What nerve. Sarah was threatening them.

Taylor turned around to face Sarah. "Why should we?" Taylor asked with her arms crossed in a tight knot. "I thought you said the Horse Club was dumb?" Taylor was on a roll! "And why hang out with the unpopular girls?"

Go girl! Kate wanted to yell. She wished she had that kind of nerve to confront the enemy without her voice breaking into pieces.

Sarah shrugged as if the motion provided a suitable answer. "Lacey is popular."

If Kate and Taylor developed a friendship with Lacey and they allowed her to join their club, would other girls consider them popular too? A twisted knot formed in Kate's belly. Did she want to be popular? A lot of pressure came with that label.

Taylor studied Kate's expression. Silently they sent a message between the two of them. Did they have a choice to turn Sarah away? They couldn't risk Layne and their parents finding out about Thunder.

"We need to have a Horse Club meeting to vote you in," Taylor explained. Little Candice was part of the club too, and the rules stated they had to all be in agreement.

"Fine, but make it fast." Sarah slid her foot into the stirrup of the saddle, and as her horse walked forward, she climbed on. Another rule of the Horse Club was for horses to stand still while mounting and dismounting. It was a safety issue. Would Sarah follow the rules, or ignore them?

Either way, Kate wanted their club to remain small. The last thing they needed was for Sarah to be a member. Lacey was bad enough. Up until now, the club members enjoyed riding together, and there was no competitive edge between them. Little Candice, the youngest member, was easy going. How would little Candice feel about the older girls taking over their club? What benefit, if any, did they add by joining the group?

Sarah's horse obviously knew his way back. While he lumbered toward the trail on a loose rein, Sarah twisted in her saddle to meet Taylor's glare. "Like I said, let me know soon. I can't keep this kind of information quiet for long."

Kate despised the pressure. Not only was Sarah rude, Kate refused to tolerate the bullying behavior. After Sarah and her horse disappeared into the woods, Kate swung around to face Taylor. "No! No way is she joining our group."

"What choice do we have?" Taylor was always so annoyingly logical.

"We can stand up to her by saying no!"

Taylor tossed up her hands. "Then what? She'll tell on us."

With that, Kate strode toward the barn. For once Taylor followed her.

The short walk didn't calm down Kate one bit. Her anger was boiling. She'd had enough of bullies pushing their way into her life and demanding their way. Even though Taylor's reasoning made sense, it did nothing to quiet Kate's anger. In fact, she was growing madder.

Kate whirled around, almost bumping into Taylor. "Then so be it if she tells," Kate said. "Do you want to hang out with Sarah all the time, ride with her, listen to her opinions in our meetings?"

"Can't say I do."

"Then we have to figure out how to keep her from joining." Kate spun back around and squinted as they entered the dim barn. Where did Lacey and Thunder go? They weren't in his stall or the aisle.

She heard Taylor's voice behind her. "Let's have a meeting tonight at my house."

"Good idea," Kate said without looking back. Taylor's house was noisier and there was less chance of being overheard, as opposed to Kate's very quiet house, where her mother knew almost everything that went on.

Kate poked her head into the tack room. No Lacey.

"Where is she?" Taylor asked, just as confused as Kate by the disappearance of rider and horse.

Kate heard someone talking at the far end of the barn aisle. There, standing in the crossties in an old wash room, was Thunder. Lacey was rinsing him off with a shabby hose.

"About time," Lacey said as if she'd been waiting forever for them to return. "I'm surprised this old hose and faucet still function. I figured Thunder deserved a good rinse because he got sweaty from that little bit of riding."

"He's out of shape," Taylor commented, avoiding Kate's scowl. "How often can you ride him?"

"Blue is still lame, so other than using different schooling horses in lessons, I can use my spare time to ride Thunder." Lacey aimed the hose at his face. He raised his head high and closed his eyes and flattened his ears to keep water from running into places he wanted to protect. It was obvious he was used to being sprayed off with water.

From his good behavior, someone owned him. But who?

"Maybe Sarah's right and we stole him," Kate said. Sarah's words haunted her mind. That old familiar guilt was becoming more than she could handle. According to her father, if you borrow something without asking, that was a form of stealing. They hadn't borrowed Thunder exactly. After all, he showed up at their barn unannounced, but they did remove him without Layne's permission, or their parents' knowledge.

"Now's a fine time to have second thoughts," Lacey barked.

Kate had thought it was a bad idea from day one. Now was no different.

"Don't let Sarah's surprise visit cause us to argue," Taylor reasoned. "That's what she wants. She put the heat on us because she's trying to bully her way into our club. Although I don't see a way around letting her join."

"When have you ever given into bullying?" Kate was sick of the conversation. She would do whatever possible to keep Sarah from joining, even if that meant telling the adults about hiding Thunder. She doubted the other girls would agree with her.

Lacey scraped off the loose water with her hand from Thunder's shiny, dark coat. "She wants to join our club?"

Our club? Kate cringed.

Taylor nodded. "She threatened to tell Layne about Thunder unless we allow her to join."

Lacey shrugged her shoulders. "That might not be so bad. She's popular, you know? Think about all the friends you'd make at school." Lacey was staring right at Kate, as if Kate needed friends.

"Oh, please." Kate said, rolling her eyes. "You think I'm desperate for friends?"

"I didn't say that. Don't be so defensive." Lacey unclipped the crossties and led Thunder back outside to graze on the fresh grass growing in large clumps in the small field.

Kate bit her tongue to keep from accusing Lacey of also forcing her way into the club. What a wonderful addition she had been so far. Sarcasm was ugly. Kate had to stop thinking that way. Instead she needed to show gratitude for all the things she was blessed with, including friends, new and old.

"We'll meet tonight at my house," Taylor said, "to vote if we want to allow Sarah into the group."

It was impossible for Kate to keep her thoughts on the subject to herself any longer. "And to vote if Lacey is allowed to join."

Lacey snapped up her head.

Kate wasn't making fast friends with Lacey or Sarah. Barn life, in addition to school, wasn't going to be easy if Kate voted against the popular girls.

CHAPTER EIGHTEEN

Kate climbed the stairs to Taylor's room, each step harder to take than the one before. Anxiety danced around in her belly similar to the first time she had met Sam at the barn. Of course, it hadn't been a date. There were other people around, but they rode together without anyone else. Tonight held the same tension. She hoped Lacey and Sarah weren't at the meeting. If they were, and if Kate spoke her mind, her popularity at school would end before she walked through the front door of the building tomorrow.

What pressure.

She argued to herself silently that it wasn't fair for people to push their popularity around. The Horse Club was supposed to be enjoyable, carefree. Kate didn't find Sarah or Lacey pleasant.

When she reached Taylor's bedroom, Candice was already sitting on the floor cross-legged, leaning against the dresser. Kate reminded herself that there was a time not that long ago that Kate disliked Candice. To be fair, the reason was mostly because Candice was leasing Kate's beloved pony, but now Kate understood the benefit of Spirit receiving twice as much love. Besides, Kate didn't have as much time for him as she used to now that she owned Razor. Spirit deserved to have the added affection of the little girl.

"Hi, Kate." Candice had the sweetest voice. The girl uncrossed her legs to shift her weight while watching Kate with admiration.

Who wouldn't love the respect written all over the young girl's face? Kate realized she did have someone who appreciated her.

Candice's admiration helped to build up Kate's confidence even if it was just a starting point. Maybe that's why Taylor had so much confidence. People loved her, adored her, and when they were with her they knew they were safe. Taylor wasn't fearful. Unlike Kate.

Taylor was leaning against the backboard of her bed with a stuffed animal, a big brown Clydesdale from her visit to St. Louis, lying across her lap. Without thinking she rubbed her hand back and forth across its fur.

Kate was more than relieved that Lacey and Sarah weren't there. She flashed her hand in the air to wave at Taylor, who didn't respond.

Taylor continued to rub the stuffed animal's

fur. Finally, looking up for the first time, she said hello to Kate.

Kate smiled in answer. She curled up next to Candice on the floor and leaned against the big dresser. "I have an hour before my mom picks me up. I have homework."

"We'll make this fast." Taylor always took the leadership role of their meetings. She was the self-appointed president of the club. "To fill you in, Candice, we have two people wanting to join the Horse Club."

"And both of them are pushing their way in uninvited." The words slipped out of Kate's mouth before she was able to stop them.

"I thought we had to vote them in." Candice crossed her arms. Apparently she didn't like people forcing their way into the Horse Club, either. "Let me guess. One of them is Lacey."

Taylor smiled, more from humor than being happy. "Exactly. And the other is Sarah."

"The tall, bossy girl?" Candice asked, frowning.

"That's her." Kate heard sarcasm layered in her own voice. She wanted to control her negative opinions more, so she didn't influence Candice one way or the other, but the task was impossible.

Candice shifted again on the floor.

"Here." Taylor tossed them each a pink decorative pillow to sit on. "The hardwood floor gets uncomfortable fast."

Kate shoved the pillow underneath her bottom. Usually she sprawled out across the foot of the bed, but today she wanted to distance herself from Taylor in case they got involved in a heavy discussion. Kate planned to voice her opinion.

"We are at a disadvantage," Taylor explained. "Sarah and Lacey both know about Thunder. If we decline their membership, we run the risk of trouble."

Candice scrunched her face in a puzzled expression.

"They'd likely tell someone." Kate had to be honest even though she disliked the idea of the girls joining their club. It was a matter of time, though, before someone found out about him. "I don't think that's a reason to make a permanent decision."

Taylor bent the Clydesdale's hoof back and forth while she processed the information. "If we don't vote them in, they will tell. How do we get around that?"

"We don't." It was Kate's turn to be the confident one.

"I'm confused." Taylor set her stuffed horse aside and tucked her knees in a ball close to her body. She wrapped her arms around them in a self-protective way. "Isn't the point of hidng Thunder at old man Brown's barn, so we can keep our secret? Otherwise Layne will send him away."

Candice spoke up. "What are you talking about? Where is he? I mean, I know you stole him."

Ouch.

"We didn't steal him," Taylor corrected. "Not exactly."

Before tonight, what had made Candice suspect they had anything to do with Thunder's disappearance?

Kate leaned toward Taylor and stared directly into her eyes. "Actually, we did steal him. He wasn't our horse, we removed him from the barn, hid him in someone else's barn, and haven't told anyone. Face it, Taylor. We took him, as in stole him."

"How can you steal something that doesn't belong to anyone?" Taylor asked.

"Someone owns him." To prove her point, Kate leaned back against the dresser again, crossing her legs. Sure, she was defensive, but at least she was correct.

Candice cleared her throat. "Whatever you call it, you're hiding him and want to keep it a secret."

Taylor swallowed hard.

"If we let these girls join, our club will change," Kate said. She despised change.

"Change isn't all that bad," Taylor said, knowing Kate well. "Sure, they aren't the girls I'd choose to join, but they might offer something fun."

Fun? Kate was doubtful.

"Why that ugly expression?" Taylor asked. "You don't even know them."

Surprised, Kate was speechless. Was Taylor starting to like Lacey? A zip of jealousy darted through her at the thought of sharing her best friend. Was Taylor accepting the bullying because she wanted to be popular? It would go without saying that people at school would notice them hanging out with Lacey and Sarah. They'd be included in the popular group automatically.

"You were less than nice to Sarah," Kate reminded Taylor. "You didn't sound like you wanted her to join." Kate remembered all too well how Taylor talked to the tall, lanky girl. She had said, *Slither away.*

"I don't want her to join, neither of them."

That confused Kate. "Then why are you encouraging us to vote them into our club?"

"I'm not. I don't see that we have a choice." Taylor was back to taking her frustration out on the poor Clydesdale she had previously set down. If she kept bending his hoof it would break open.

"Wait a minute," Candice said, still sitting in the exact same position on the pillow. "You don't want them voted in, but because you're afraid they might tell about Thunder, you are willing to allow them to join our club in order to keep them quiet? They are older than us, a lot older than me. We have nothing in common except horses."

"Isn't that enough?" Taylor asked with a raised tone as if to ask what age had to do with anything. "That's the point of the Horse Club."

"They are all about boys and being popular," Candice explained, sounding far older than she was. "I don't care about those things yet."

Kate cared about boys too much. Still, that wasn't a reason to change her mind about voting the girls into the club.

"What do boys have to do with horses?" Taylor asked, pressing Candice for more information.

"My mom will have a fit if boys are involved in our sleepovers, or our trail rides. She won't let me go." Candice's lip puckered. "She trusts you both, not Lacey and Sarah."

Point taken. Kate didn't trust them, either. Lacey was already chasing after Sam.

"How do we solve this?" Taylor asked. At least she was open to suggestions.

"Make a second club." Sometimes Candice, who didn't speak much in general, had wonderful ideas.

Taylor's eyebrows raised. "Tell me more."

"Instead of just having the Horse Club, make a jumping club too." Candice finally moved around on the pillow, uncrossing her legs and stretching them outward. "They can join that club with you. At some point you're going to want to hang out with older kids. When that happens, I can find younger riders to continue with the Horse Club."

"I don't want to leave the Horse Club," Kate said, emotion filling her voice.

"You don't have to quit," Candice reasoned. "Stay in the Horse Club but ride with them too."

What she said made sense.

"That way, when you outgrow the Horse Club, you have another one."

"I mean why would we outgrow the Horse Club?" Taylor asked, a puzzled look on her face.

"Look at our ages," Candice said.

Kate understood more than anyone else about the age differences between all of them. "I like the idea of the Horse club focusing on riding in general, and a jumping club honing in on jumping. Two clubs offer an opportunity to zoom in on different things but yet work together."

"Exactly," Candice said. "I'm not at your riding level."

"But we love you," Kate said, surprised by her tender feelings toward the girl. "I'll miss you."

"Thanks." Candice's smile grew wide. "Look at how you're already doing things with older girls, like hiding Thunder with them. For a couple of weeks now I've been riding with girls my own age. I take lessons with them, and you take lessons with Lacey."

Kate frowned at the mention of Lacey's name.

"She's not so bad," Taylor said.

"Why do you always stick up for her?" Kate demanded. "Is she becoming your new best friend?"

Taylor rolled her eyes. "So that's the problem. You're jealous."

"No! Of course not." Or was she? "Well, maybe a little." At least Kate was being honest.

Candice's eyes widened.

"You have nothing to worry about," Taylor said, reassuring her. "You'll always be my best friend."

Kate relaxed somewhat. She hadn't realized she was squeezing her knees tightly together until her left leg fell asleep. She stood to shake it out. "You're my best friend too." After she said the words, she worried about Candice's feelings. "I didn't mean to leave you out, Candice. You're one of my best friends too."

Candice tossed her head back and laughed, bumping it on the dresser. "I know." She rubbed the back of her head with her hand.

"So if we start a jumping club," Taylor said, "we'd ask Lacey and Sarah to join and everyone will be happy. We have our Horse Club still with the three of us, so we are happy, and they're happy because they belong to a jumping club."

As Kate's dad always said during an argument, try for a win-win result to make everyone happy. "Think they'll keep our secret?" Kate asked.

Taylor shrugged. "We can only hope."

CHAPTER NINETEEN

"A jumping club?" Lacey asked. They were standing in the aisle of the lower barn where the older girls hung out.

Sarah didn't say anything. Kate couldn't read her expression, either.

"Yes," Taylor said. "It's the same as the Horse Club but for older girls who are working on jumping and horseshows."

"That sounds fun," Lacey said. "No offense, but Candice is a little young for us."

Kate stood taller. So help her, if anyone said anything negative about Candice they would hear an earful.

Lacey seemed to notice Kate's body language and backed off. "I think it's a great idea. It makes sense."

Sarah remained quiet, her thoughts important because she was the reason they had to make a new club to begin with.

"Well," Taylor pushed, staring at Sarah. The pressure was on.

Sarah was leaning against her horse's stall door. He was trying to nuzzle her hair through the bars but she ignored him. "I love the idea."

Thank goodness. Did that mean she would keep the secret? Kate wasn't about to ask.

"I expect that you'll keep the topic of Thunder between us," Taylor said. Not only was she brave for asking, she was the best at being direct.

"Sure." Sarah pulled away from the stall and slid open the door. "Do you hear that, Bagel? We're going to be members of a jumping club." He nickered at the sound of her voice. "Bagel likes the idea too."

Again, Kate wondered if Sarah wasn't as confident as she let on. Sure, she was part of the popular group of girls at school, but yet she was excited to join the jumping club. It amazed Kate to think they had something the popular girls wanted to be a part of. Was everyone, popular or not, striving for social acceptance? What an interesting concept.

Shifting her focus back to the subject at hand, Kate said, "We need a better name for the jumping club." Starting another club meant more work, but she appreciated Candice's smart idea even more now. Both Lacey and Sarah seemed to like the idea. Not only was the thought brilliant, it helped preserve the Horse Club from more change than Kate wanted.

"What's wrong with the name?" Taylor asked, a little prickly sounding.

Kate wondered why but it wasn't worth asking in front of everyone.

"The name is boring," Lacey said. "How about Awesome Jump Club."

Kate laughed. "How about Horseshoe Jumping Club, named after Horseshoe River. That reminds me of one of our most memorable trail rides."

"Love it," Sarah said. "Why was it memorable?"

Taylor chuckled, obviously remembering the most adventurous ride they'd ever had.

"Let's just say, we won't try swimming in Horseshoe River again," Kate said. "That was the scariest ride of my life."

"Nothing but trail trouble that day," Taylor agreed. "Let's vote. All in favor of Horseshoe Jumping Club raise their hands."

All four girls raised their hands. They actually agreed on something together, a positive sign.

"Let's start the club off right and ride together," Sarah said.

Again, Kate found Sarah's desire to be included interesting. Kate always thought the popular girls had people wanting to join their groups instead of the other way around. That thought made Sarah and Lacey seem less scary, less intimidating.

Confidence. Kate's confidence was increasing.

Life seemed to circle around that one word.

Kate's mind shifted to Candice. Kate didn't want to leave her out again by riding with the older girls. By starting the new club, they needed to be careful not to hurt anyone's feelings. Candice was right, there were problems with including the older girls with the younger ones. Kate and Taylor were caught in that awkward, in-between age.

Sarah pulled her horse from the stall and cross tied him in the aisle.

"I wish I had Thunder to ride," Lacey complained. She was also caught in an awkward stage. All the girls at the barn owned their own horses, or in Candice's case she leased Spirit, but not Lacey. Lacey rode a schooling horse. And Blue was lame. How was she supposed to ride spontaneously if she didn't own a horse?

Kate disliked Lacey a lot, she would even go as far to say the other girl was a bully, but as Kate got to know her, she had to admit that Lacey had a likeable side. Then Kate remembered Lacey going to the mall with Sam. A flash of anger coursed through her body. Her dad would say that Lacey was insecure. She needed the attention of other people's boyfriends for her to feel accepted and secure in life.

When Kate viewed Lacey's behavior from the angle that the other girl was insecure, Kate became more understanding and not as threatened. It wasn't a personal attack on Kate but was about Lacey needing attention. Actually, that thought eased Kate's anger significantly, and to her surprise, made Kate want to help Lacey.

"I have an idea," Kate said from a place of caring. "Why don't you share Razor with me?" It could be an example of a win-win situation. Lacey was a good rider and Razor would benefit.

Taylor's mouth dropped open. She stared at Kate as if she had gone crazy.

Lacey's mouth gaped open as well. "No offense Kate, but I didn't think you liked me."

How was Kate supposed to answer? She decided that no words described the change of heart she'd had, so she smiled instead. "If you want to share with me, that's fine. Meet me in the ring." Kate whirled around on her boot heels and strode with confidence—yes, confidence—to the upper barn to check on Candice.

When she reached Candice, she had Spirit cross tied in the aisle with several other ponies. Kate recognized two of the girls.

"Kate!" Candice bounced up to Kate and slid an arm around her.

Joy filled her. She loved the little girl's excitement. One thing about Candice, she always made Kate feel important. An observation that Kate made was that older kids in general seemed to to keep a distance from the younger kids because they had a reputation to uphold. It was sad really. There was so much pleasure in hanging out with the younger crowd, and less drama and social pressure. Did Kate really want to step up to the older group of girls? Did she have to choose, or could she hold onto both?

One of the girls Kate recognized but didn't know her name bounced up to Kate. "Hi. Will you help me tighten my girth? I can't get it."

Kate smiled, her heart filling with warmth. Helping the girls meant a lot to her and she never realized that before now. "Sure." Kate followed the bouncing girl back to her pony.

She tightened girths, put on bridles, and fastened a helmet. Helping others filled her heart with love and *confidence*. Kate smiled to herself. That word seemed to be her lesson in life right now.

After the girls left the barn with their horses, Kate pulled out Razor. Dried mud covered his coat from head to toe from rolling in the turnout and would take longer than she had planned to brush him. Normally she didn't mind. She enjoyed spending time with him, but today her friends were waiting. As she thought about her friends, new and old, Taylor appeared at the backlit entrance to the barn, looking taller, more mature. Kate had to squint to make sure it was her. They were growing up faster than Kate wanted.

With the sunlight dancing in her hair, Lacey, a good head taller, strode in behind Taylor.

Kate knew she had grown too. Most of her clothes were either tighter or shorter. Somehow they had grown up overnight. Even her emotions felt different, a combination of maturity and responsibility, mixed with vibrancy and irresponsibility. How confusing her life was from minute to minute. Kate wasn't sure she wanted all this change.

She ran a brush along Razor's back, knocking off clumps of dried dirt. Usually brushing him alone allowed her time to think about people, school, the barn, and filled her with love for Razor. If asked by non-horse people, she could never explain the sense of joy she received from her relationship with her horse. He always knew when she was having a good day, a bad day, or in need of someone to hear her frustrations. Razor was her best friend.

"Can I help brush him?" Lacey's voice broke through Kate's deep thoughts.

"Sure." A week ago Kate couldn't imagine allowing Lacey to help. More change, positive change that she invited.

Lacey brushed one side of Razor while Kate brushed the other. When Kate was finished she took Razor's hair brush and worked on his still thick but shorter mane. Kate was grateful her mother had spent time pulling it along with clipping his legs and muzzle.

She made a mental note to spend tomorrow giving her own horse attention instead caring for Thunder. He was a priority.

Kate tossed the hair brush back into the neon-green grooming bucket she'd begged her mother to buy. Kate loved anything neon. She headed into the tack room, surprised when Lacey followed.

"If I'm going to ride, let me carry the saddle and whatever else you need." Lacey wanted to help. Wow.

The thought of sharing Razor was a challenge, one that Kate hadn't dealt well with when she'd first leased Spirit to Candice, but Kate reminded herself that she had learned that lesson in a positive way. Sharing had been difficult at first, downright painful even, but Kate had survived. Giving to others was a sacrifice her dad always said expanded your heart to receive love back. If sharing wasn't tough, then giving wouldn't be rewarding. It was hard to admit, but her dad was right.

That brought her thoughts back to Lacey. She didn't have her own horse, which made Kate remember to appreciate Razor. In the past she'd viewed Lacey as having everything. She had gorgeous hair, an athletic body, a killer smile, tons of friends, and guys loved her. But she didn't have a horse as a best friend. That was powerful.

Kate wouldn't trade all the other stuff for Razor. No way.

Today was a day for interesting thoughts.

Kate pulled her saddle, girth, and pad off the rack from her locker and handed them to Lacey, who seemed to be learning the lesson of giving too. She accepted it gratefully and disappeared out of the tack room. Life was interesting, for sure. Kate looped the bridle over her shoulder, grabbed her helmet and crop, and followed Lacey out the door.

Together they tacked up Razor. Taylor was in the set of crossties behind them, watching quietly. Was she jealous? No, she was probably surprised by the fact that Kate and Lacey were getting along, and observing the teamwork between them.

When finished, they led the horses outside to the mounting block. Kate climbed on Razor first. She would warm him up and then let Lacey ride. As long as Lacey didn't jump him, because Kate was working on certain techniques that Layne was teaching her, Kate was willing to share.

As they entered the ring, Kate noticed again the age difference between the smaller girls riding in Candice's lesson compared to the group of girls Kate rode with to the arena. Candice was right, the group as a whole wouldn't work, but two clubs worked perfectly, even if Kate and Taylor belonged to both. Kate thought of the benefits, such as offering each other help and experiences they'd otherwise miss.

The younger kids were fun, free from responsibility, and the older kids had a chance to mentor them. Riding together was enjoyable.

Kate pushed Razor forward during their warm up. He was naturally lazy, needing a lot of encouragement. If he had the choice, he would stop at any opportunity to sneak a rest break. Today was warm, but hotter days offered more of a challenge because he was even lazier. Kate wasn't complaining because she far preferred to push him forward than to have him revved up and spooking. His calm attitude helped build Kate's level of trust in riding.

After she warmed him up with Lacey watching, Kate dismounted. She handed over the reins of her beloved horse to the girl who stole a date with Sam. Despite how it sounded, the act felt refreshing.

Lacey climbed on him. Would she enjoy him, appreciate him? Kate realized she was worried about Lacey's opinion again, and about what she'd say to the kids at school. Silently Kate scolded herself. She needed to stop caring about what other people thought. Why was that so difficult?

Not at all surprising, Lacey rode Razor well. He was calm and responsive, and she fit his size, but when she rode Thunder they looked amazing. There was something electric about the pair that was unstoppable.

Secretly, the competitive side of Kate was glad she didn't have to compete against Lacey and Thunder.

CHAPTER TWENTY

Thunder whinnied when he saw the girls.

Even though Lacey rode him almost daily, it was obvious that the horse missed having another equine companion. He had developed the habit of pacing back and forth in his stall, and had become obnoxious with desire for attention by rubbing his face against the girls, pushing into their space as if starved for affection. He had even started trying to barge out of the stall as soon as they opened the door.

Horses were herd animals and needed grazing time in the field with other horses. It wasn't enough that the girls took care of him twice a day and worked him in the limited area available. They had tried to expand the riding area once by having Lacey take him on a short trail ride with the girls walking alongside him for company to keep him calm. He behaved well even though he didn't have another horse along, but the fear of being seen or heard by someone was far too great. He had whinnied several times. One thing was for certain: Thunder needed other horses.

The truth of the situation stared them in the face. Someone owned him and they couldn't continue this level of care.

It was possible that if had he gone to the rescue as planned, he would be reunited with his original owner by now. Had they interfered with him returning home? The answer was yes.

"He seems sad," Lacey said, stroking his face. "He misses being at a barn full of horses."

Kate didn't blame him. She knew all too well how lonely it was to be the only child living at home. Often Taylor spent the night because she enjoyed the quiet of Kate's house. Taylor's house was full of noise, with having twins as siblings, but even though she complained occasionally, Kate knew her friend loved having a larger family. People as well as horses were made to have friends.

"What are we going to do?" Kate asked. She slid open his stall door, and instead of trying to barge through, he greeted her by burying his face in her chest. She allowed her to rub his ears, even the insides of them. Someone had trained him well because horses usually reacted to their ears being touched.

Taylor squeezed past them to enter the stall. She leaned against the near wall and shrugged in defeat. "What can we do? We can't tell anyone, but yet Thunder needs horse friends."

Sarah and Lacey stood in the doorway, Lacey leaning against the frame. Neither girl had any suggestions. Their faces were blank with uncertainty.

Kate continued to rub Thunder's ears while pondering Taylor's question. What would her dad advise? Without a doubt he'd recommend doing the right thing by admitting they made a mistake, so it could be fixed.

But their parents would ground them for life.

Kate ran her hands down his face to play with his muzzle. "Think we'd be grounded for less time if we came forward?"

Taylor's eyes widened with alarm. When she caught her breath, she said, "You aren't thinking about coming clean are you?"

Kate turned her head away from Taylor's intense glare.

"Kate?" Lacey asked. "If you say something, we all get in trouble."

Kate was sick of peer pressure. "We need to think about Thunder, not ourselves. He's getting depressed."

Lacey ran her hand through her long hair before she answered. She was a slow thinker, which Kate appreciated.

"I want to go to the upcoming dance," Lacey

said. "While I'm concerned about Thunder, telling our parents is not an option." The weight of her words carried the promise of threat.

Kate's belly knotted. She wanted out of this mess.

"I want to go to the dance too," Taylor said. Cute Josh Thompson had asked her. They had actually started dating, if you could call it that at their age, at the last Valentine's dance.

Why hadn't Sam asked Kate to the upcoming dance yet? The knot in Kate's belly grew bigger and tighter. "Who are you going to the dance with, Lacey?"

Lacey's face turned the color of a red-delicious apple.

"Oh, no you're not!" Kate clenched her jaw shut. That little … little…brat.

Lacey stepped to the side of the stall door, so Kate had only a minimal view of the left side of her body. Traitor!

Taylor pushed off the wall so abruptly that Thunder spooked and darted back. "You're going with Sam, as in Kate's Sam? That is low."

Lacey pushed away from the wall as if she wanted to run out of the barn. She turned her head away.

"Horse Club members don't date other members' boyfriends." Taylor's voice shook from anger.

Sarah spoke up. "Technically we aren't members of the Horse Club. You started a jumping club and we haven't discussed the rules yet."

Taylor whipped around to face Sarah. "Excuse me? Friends don't do that. If you aren't a friend, then leave the club."

"I know too much to walk away." Apparently not intimidated, Sarah glared back at Taylor. "I will tell. Simple as that."

Taylor thrusted her index finger toward Sarah's face. "Then tell. I'm sick of your threats. In fact, I'm sick of you both having no compassion or respect for anyone else. If that's how you are, then leave. Now!"

Sarah and Lacey hurried away. Kate heard one of them bump into the half-closed barn door as they exited.

Neither Kate nor Taylor spoke for an extended period. When Kate broke the silence her voice was shaky. "Now what are we going to do? Thunder is depressed, the adults will find out about him, and we're stuck in this alone."

Taylor remained quiet. Her gaze held that far-away look that said she was lost in deep thought. Kate didn't disturb her and allowed her to finish processing her thoughts. Taylor was smart. She would come up with a plan. If not, Kate was twirling around an idea in her own mind, but one Taylor was sure to hate.

When Kate could no longer stand the quiet, she spoke up first. "I think we should come clean. Either way we're going to get in trouble." She inhaled three long breaths, once again practicing Layne's well-appreciated technique, and then continued to reason with Taylor. "It'll be less of a punishment if we tell someone."

Taylor snapped her head upward, her distant gaze clearing instantly. She met Kate's eye contact without wavering. "That's a horrible idea."

Kate choked down a lump of emotion forming in her throat. Her best friend wasn't usually so gruff. There were times where she was direct, but she was acting downright rude. Kate tried to remember her father's wise words. *Don't take people's reactions personally. It's a reflection about them, not you.* In other words, Taylor's reaction had nothing to do with Kate. She was afraid, concerned about the punishment her parents would force upon her.

A sense of peace, no matter how temporary, filled Kate. They needed to work together as a team to figure out what to do about Thunder. After all, they had locked him up in a secluded barn to hide them from their parents, and to prevent him from going to a horse rescue. Was that love?

Kate rubbed his face. He lowered his head to allow her to rub behind his ears. "He's sad, Taylor. We have to do something."

Taylor's face lit up. "Why don't we open the paddock door so he can roam outside. I don't blame him for being depressed. He's locked in this stall all the time."

"His paddock is a mess. We'd have to clean it up so he'd be safe." Kate liked the idea but still thought they should be honest and tell their parents instead of delay the inevitable. Their parents would find out soon enough.

"We can work on his paddock today," Taylor said, rocking her foot back and forth as she leaned against the stall door. "I don't think old man Brown will see him if we turn him out."

"Unless he whinnies."

Taylor didn't respond. Ignoring the truth, she stood up straight, ready to take action. "We don't have a choice. He needs to be outside and this is a quick fix." When Taylor got her mind set on something, she didn't let go easily.

Even though Kate disagreed with the plan, as usual, she went along with it to keep peace. Conflict wasn't her thing.

"Let's get busy then," Taylor suggested. I'll go around back and open the stall door, and you find our work gloves in the feed room. We have a lot to do."

Kate slid her hand down Thunder's long nose one last time before she set off to find the gloves. She reminded herself that all this hard work was for him. If he had to be hidden, he deserved a happy life. There was no doubt he'd enjoy being outside during good weather. If today went well Kate planned to suggest he stay out at night too.

She found the gloves on a dusty shelf. Lacey must have set them there. Just thinking about her brought the anger back. Kate needed to let the stress go. If Sam wanted to take Lacey to the dance, then they deserved each other.

Taylor's voice drifted into the feed room. "Can you bring the hammer and box of nails?"

Kate searched the dim feed room for the supplies. On another wooden shelf she found the hammer and nails, a thin layer of dust covering them.

She carried the supplies through the barn and cut through Thunder's stall. Taylor had opened the split window door from the outside and Thunder stood in the doorway looking out with curiosity. He didn't dare step foot into the overgrown paddock. The weeds claimed most of the small area.

Kate tossed Taylor, who had already started pulling the weeds with her bare hands, a pair of blue flowered gloves. "Use these. You'll tear your hands up fast without them."

She set the hammer and nails down in the corner of the paddock, and then slapped a pair of dusty, pretty pink flowered gloves against her leg to knock off a coating of dirt. She sneezed three times before pulling them on.

Kate glanced around the paddock. The weeds were thicker than she at first thought.

If Sarah did tell the adults, all this work was for nothing. Not wanting to be a downer, Kate wrapped her hands around the base of a tall weed and yanked. When the weed didn't budge, she braced her legs and gave another hard pull. Part of the weed escaped the packed clay but the other half remained rooted.

"Why don't we wet the ground first with the hose?" Taylor asked while she tugged at her own clump of stubborn weeds.

"Great idea. I'll get it," Kate offered. Instead of going all the way around the front of the barn, or interrupting Thunder, who was standing in the doorway of his stall watching them, she slid through the wooden fence and entered the back of the barn. They had left the barn door cracked open to offer Thunder fresh air. It wasn't healthy for him to breathe the dusty old barn air.

The best she could, she tried to untangle the hose knotted in a bundle in the wash room. When the majority of it was loose she turned on the faucet. The rest of the hose unraveled as she dragged it around the back of the barn.

To avoid spraying Taylor, Kate aimed a stream of water at the base of the weed near her friend's feet. The ground was so dry it soaked up the liquid almost as fast as the water wet the dirt. She would have to spray one section at a time. At this rate the job at hand might take a while.

"Try that now," Kate said.

Taylor tugged at the clump of weeds. It resisted at first but then parted from the earth in one bundle. "Whoop! It worked!"

"That will save some time," Kate said, thankful the barn had a working water spigot and hose. When the back corner was finally muddy, Kate twisted the sprayer closed and set down the hose. She pulled at a section of weeds, surprised by the ease in which the clump loosened.

Every so often Kate soaked another small section of ground. For the next hour they pulled weeds until the paddock was clear enough for Thunder to safely walk around without fear of stepping on a snake or entangling his legs.

Taylor tossed the last clump of weeds over the railing. "I need to fix a few fence boards first."

Kate passed her the hammer and nails from the corner of the paddock.

When they finished, exhausted, Kate stopped to admire their handiwork. "Looks pretty good," she said. Apparently Thunder agreed. He stretched his neck farther out the door to sniff the fresh air. Kate and Taylor chuckled.

"Why won't he step out?" Kate asked, confused.

"It's something new." Taylor tugged on his mane to encourage him to walk through the doorway. He took one hesitant step, and then another.

"Let's leave him out here tonight so he can stretch his legs," Kate suggested. "He deserves freedom."

"I agree," Taylor said. "I don't think anything will go wrong."

Thunder tiptoed around the paddock, sniffing every inch. He was so cautious, Kate had to wonder why. Did he sense something they weren't aware of?

CHAPTER TWENTY-ONE

Kate woke up in the middle of the night to a raging thunderstorm. The lightning lit up her room, the crack of thunder sending her under her quilt.

Her bed was safe. Yes, safe. She was too old to run to her mother's room to crawl into bed with her. She resisted the urge and grabbed hold of her stuffie instead. The worn dog had offered her comfort many times in the past, especially lately with the guilt she carried over hiding Thunder.

Thunder!

He was outside in this weather without the safety of being closed in his stall. She hoped he had enough sense to stay inside and out of the dangerous lightning. Then she remembered the night they had found him. He was running loose through a storm just like this one. Lightning and thunder hadn't kept him inside that time.

She gasped at the thought. It was late, too dangerous to creep out of bed to check on him. Was he scared? Lightning lit up her room again. Against her better judgment, against a strong urge to crawl deeper under her covers, Kate faced her fear of the storm and slid out of bed. Thunder was not only her responsibility, at least in part, but he was important to her.

The house was quiet, too quiet, until the hallway filled with a flash of light spilling in from the window. Sure enough, a crack of thunder followed. Kate shook in her pajamas. It wasn't until the second crack that sent her running back to the safety of her bed. She dove under her covers. Stuffie dog was waiting to comfort her.

For a moment, when her own fear took over, all thoughts of the horse vanished. *Breathe, just breathe.* She'd never been hurt before in a storm, nor did the likelihood of this one pose a threat.

After she relaxed somewhat from the comfort of the soft stuffed animal in her arms, a vision of the horse, most likely running around scared, returned to her mind. He was probably afraid, shaking just like Kate had before she climbed back under the covers. Thunder had no one, no other horses or people, to help keep him calm. Horses were herd animals. He was alone, hidden in a barn reclaimed by the dark, scary woods, in a major lightning storm. Poor guy.

He needed comfort, but the thought of leaving her bed made her curl up under the quilt and squeeze her stuffie even more. Thunder would have to wait until morning. She wasn't about to risk her life, her safety, by venturing out in the storm. It was far too frightening.

Kate wanted to call Taylor. She peeked out from the edge of the blanket to glance at the clock radio, but the time was flashing red numbers. The electricity had blinked off. There was no way of knowing the time without venturing downstairs to look at the battery-operated clock, more of a decoration than a time-telling device, hanging on their living room wall. No thanks.

The visions of Thunder scared, running around, continued to haunt Kate. Guilt overcame her. Finally, without trying to reason the risks involved, she climbed from the safety of her comfortable bed, slipped on socks, and made her way down the steps. The big old clock read four o'clock in the morning. Her parents were early rises and would be waking up soon.

The rain pounded against the window. Kate's mother kept raincoats and umbrellas organized in the coat closet under the steps. Kate made her way to the closet in the dark to pull out one of each. Her muck boots waited by the backdoor, and still in her pajamas, she slipped her feet into them. She tried hard not to make a noise, but as soon as she opened the backdoor, it squeaked loud enough to echo through the quiet house. The last thing she wanted was to wake up her parents.

Before she stepped outside, she remembered to tiptoe back across the kitchen floor to snatch a flashlight out of the utility drawer. She wasn't about to get lost on the trail in the dark again, in a thunderstorm, nonetheless. As she closed the utility drawer, lightning lit up the kitchen as if it were daylight. Kate counted to three seconds until the crack of thunder followed. The storm was almost overhead.

She crept onto the deck and shut the door quietly behind her. Thank goodness they had a small overhang just outside the door, otherwise she'd be already drenched. Kate pulled the rain poncho over her head. The umbrella opened easily, offering a wide span of protection from the downpour once she stepped away from the overhang.

Yet another trip to the barn at night, another adventure. A jagged flash of lightning lit up the sky followed by a loud clap of ear-splitting thunder. She fought the urge to run back inside and hide under her quilt. Was she crazy to walk outside in a storm? If her mother allowed her to own a cell phone she'd call Taylor for company. She would prefer not to venture out alone with no one meeting her at the barn.

Breathe. One breath, two breaths, three breaths. A flash of light, a clap of thunder intensified her fear. *Just place one step after another.*

She picked up her pace and practically ran down the street. Shiny wet pavement lit up from the lightning. With luck no one would be glancing out their windows this early in the morning. She entered the dark woods at the trail head. It was difficult to see but she managed to pick her way down the slippery hill next to a neighbor's house. She grabbed hold of several overhanging tree branches to keep from falling. Another crack of thunder shook her insides. She needed to hurry to the barn to get out of the storm but the wet ground forced her to remain slow and steady. She would be there soon enough.

Alone.

Kate despised the thought of being at the old barn alone. She wished more than anything that Taylor was meeting her there. Kate's father always said to pray for what you want, and if it was meant to be, your wish would attract the very thing you desired. Kate found that hard to believe, but she had to admit, the several times she had tried her father's advice, she received the general idea of what she'd asked for. Well, there was no time like the present to test out her father's advice again.

Please, oh please, let someone be at old man Brown's barn tonight.

Did she need to be more specific? She would

hate for just anyone to show up. *Please let Taylor be at the barn tonight.* That was better, a more direct request.

The lightning lit up the trail ahead. She had already reached the turn off that lead to old man Brown's hidden barn. But something seemed "off." At first glance the old barn looked the same as they had left it earlier that night. Except a light was on inside the barn.

Kate gasped. Who had turned a light on, and why? She was sure all the lights were off when they had left, mostly because they never turned them on to begin with, as not to risk old man Brown noticing the light through the trees if he glanced out his back window.

On guard, she crept closer.

There, standing in Thunder's doorway leading to his paddock was a dark shadow of a person. Taylor? Kate's heart rate sped up even faster. Had Lacey and Sarah told the adults about Thunder?

Kate stayed in the dark shadow of the trees. As soon as the next streak of lightning lit up the area she realized that hiding was impossible. The object in the doorway stared in her direction. It was Taylor! Kate's father was right. She attracted what she prayed for.

Kate took a few steps forward, still somewhat cautious. "I'm so happy to see you," she said. If ever there had been a time she was relieved to see

Taylor, it was now. But from Taylor's rigid posture she knew her friend wasn't smiling.

A much taller shadow walked up behind her friend. Kate gulped. Until the sky lit up again, the person staring in her direction remained a mystery.

Kate froze in place, her mind swirling.

The lightning, farther off in the distance now, lit up the sky enough to reveal who was standing behind Taylor. Kate gasped. Old man Brown!

He stared directly at Kate.

"What are you girls up to?" the old man asked. "Why are you snooping around my barn in the middle of the night?"

He didn't know?

Confused, Kate didn't answer.

Then she realized she was standing near the paddock fence and Thunder wasn't there. Was he in his stall?

Lightning flickered like fireworks in the sky. That was when Kate noticed the broken fence on the far side of the paddock. Thunder was gone!

CHAPTER TWENTY-TWO

Curious about Thunder, Kate wanted to run past old man Brown and into the barn to look for the horse, but her legs were heavy like lead, weighted to the ground where she stood frozen. Certainly, Thunder was nowhere around. Had the storm scared him off? Had he jumped out of the paddock when the overhead thunder had cracked so loudly it rattled her own soul?

The first night they met Thunder was during a storm a lot like this one. He had galloped across the asphalt, lightning illuminating his path, as he ran through the barn doors to where the girls stood. Had he escaped his real home by jumping the paddock fence during that storm? Things were starting to make sense.

The old man disappeared for a moment. Another light in the barn flipped on along with a flood light hanging on the far corner near the roofline.

Kate had the opportunity to run back into the woods. He would never catch up with her. He wouldn't know who she was. She knew Taylor would want her to escape, but she wasn't about to leave her best friend behind to deal with the man alone.

When he returned to the doorway behind Taylor, he crossed his arms.

"Why are you girls in my barn?" old man Brown asked again, his voice gruff.

He didn't know about Thunder.

Neither girl answered.

"It's late. Why are you out in this weather?" he asked. "Answer me, or I'll call your parents."

He'd probably call them anyway. Both girls remained silent. Besides, he didn't have their parents' phone numbers, didn't even know their names.

"Fine, I'll call Layne. I'm sure she'd be interested to know two of her barn kids are hiding a horse on my property."

Kate gulped. So he did know about Thunder. Kate's knees were shaking even though her feet were still planted in place. She needed to sit down but didn't dare move.

"I want to know why you're here? Why the secret?"

Taylor spoke up. "He's a runaway. We were trying to save him from going to a rescue."

The truth sounded noble, at least to Kate.

Old man Brown's stern face, highlighted from the dim barn light, refused to soften. Apparently he didn't think the act was a noble one.

"There is nothing wrong with a rescue," he said. His face looked like stone, rigid and cold in the dim light. "At least horses get the proper care."

Was he implying they weren't taking good care of Thunder?

"Your horse jumped the fence," he continued to say. "I was watching the storm from my window. Lightning lit up my old barn, and I saw this big horse clear the fence. You can imagine my surprise."

"Sorry, sir," Taylor said, her voice shaking as if she were scared to talk to the man. Kate didn't blame her. He was downright frightening.

The man shrugged off her apology. "I appreciate you caring for him, trying to save him. Not many young people care enough to prioritize animals anymore."

If he understood, would he take their side and not call their parents?

"The question is," he asked, "where did your horse go?"

Kate relaxed a little. Maybe old man Brown was friendlier than she had thought.

"I don't know," Taylor said, taking a step closer to Kate. "That's how we found him. He was running wild during a storm. Guess he doesn't like them."

"Horses usually return home," he said. "But where is home?"

Thunder was lost to begin with. Or was he? They never gave him a chance to leave their presence once they found him.

"Home…" Taylor repeated, and then her eyes widened. "Our barn!"

If he returned to the main barn, there was a good chance someone would see him. Layne showed up often during the night to check on the horses, especially in bad weather.

"We need to call your parents," old man Brown said. "Have them meet us at the barn. You can ride with me."

A chill ran through Kate, seemingly freezing every cell in her body. There was no way Kate planned to sit in a car with a man she didn't know. Her mom always told her not to ride with strangers. How were they going to get out of this mess?

"Second thought," old man Brown said as if reading Kate's mind, "give them my address and they can pick you up here."

While that was a better scenario than riding with him, Kate resisted calling her parents. "Um, they don't know we're out here."

"Mine, either," Taylor said.

Old man Brown rubbed his chin as if he were

thinking. Why did tonight have to be so difficult? All Kate wanted to do was crawl back into bed under the safety of her quilt.

"Call them," old man Brown said again. His frown deepened.

Kate and Taylor glanced at each other. "We don't have cell phones," Taylor explained.

If his scrunched eyebrows meant anything, it likely meant he didn't believe they didn't own a cell phone. It was true, most kids seemed to have one. Unfortunately, Kate's mom refused to listen to that constant argument.

He dug his cell from the pocket of his jeans. "No problem. Give me phone numbers."

Again, neither girl spoke.

"Now," he commanded.

Kate and Taylor mumbled their phone numbers at the same time. How he understood them was beyond her.

To Kate's disappointment, he dialed her mom's number first. From where Kate's feet were still planted, she had no trouble overhearing her mother's loud response.

"Yes, I have your daughter at my barn," he said twice, probably because her mother thought the call was a prank. "David Brown. I live on Canter Lane."

More loud speaking but Kate wasn't able to decipher what her mother was saying. Whatever her words, she didn't sound happy.

"They're at my house," he explained. "It's a long story. I'd prefer to discuss it when you pick them up." He nodded as if Kate's mom could see him. "Okay, ten minutes." He clicked off the phone and shoved it deep into the right pocket of his jeans. The thunder cracked off in the distance.

Kate watched old man Brown but his highlighted face, illuminated at an angle by the floodlight, revealed no hint as to how her mother took the news.

He noticed her watching him. As if he read her mind once again he said, "She's not happy." Kate and Taylor continued to stare at him. "She's calling your friend's mom," he said, pointing to Taylor.

Taylor slumped her shoulders, also highlighted by the wide berth of the floodlight. After all the hard work, their secret was out. They were about to face their parents. She and Taylor would be in big trouble. And Lacy, nor Sarah, would likely be found out.

CHAPTER TWENTY-THREE

The crunch of tires sounded from a car on old man Brown's gravel driveway. The vehicle skidded to a stop. Kate resisted the urge to hide and wished it possible to disappear. They were now waiting outside old man Barown's house.

Unfortunately, the car belonged to her mother. The driver's door slammed in perfect beat with Kate's pounding heart. The passenger door slammed next. The beam of the unwanted floodlight revealed Taylor's mom as the passenger. They were in double trouble.

Kate's mom stormed toward them with Taylor's mom close behind. Just then another car pulled into the driveway. Kate's dad. That could be good and bad. While he was reasonable, where as Kate's mom tended to overreact, he was also stricter. His punishments were harsher and lasted longer.

Her mother, still dressed in designer pajama

pants and a workout top, stopped directly in front of the girls. She didn't pause long enough to notice old man Brown. "Kate. What were you thinking sneaking out in the middle of the night? What's wrong with you?"

"In a storm, nonetheless," Taylor's mom added.

Neither girl dared to answer. It wasn't really a question anyway as much as it was an accusation.

Kate's dad joined them. He was calm, dressed in jeans and a long-sleeved, collared shirt. If she didn't know it wasn't early morning, she would assume he was going to a casual dinner to meet friends. He always dressed nice, apparently even before the birds woke up.

"Kate," he said in his deep voice, one that Kate never attempted to argue with. "I'm sure you can explain what you and Taylor are doing out here, keeping this kind man from his sleep."

Kate's mouth went dry. What she wouldn't give for a bottle of water. And did he have to be so logical always, as if attending a meeting?

He knew to wait for her mind to process what he asked. When she swallowed hard, she managed to squeak out a reply. "It's a long story, Dad."

He didn't answer. That was part of his trick to guilt her into talking more, and her mom always stood by quietly and let him. As usual, the trick worked.

Kate inhaled slowly before she was able to

speak. "A horse showed up one night when we were at the barn." Kate shifted her weight back and forth from nervous energy. "It was storming like it is tonight. We kept him for a while but Layne wanted to turn him over to her friend who runs a horse rescue."

Still no answer, no reply from anyone. Kate was used to Taylor taking the lead, but tonight was her turn.

"We thought the rescue was a horrible idea, plus we fell in love with him." Kate knew that the honest truth was her best shot at trying to make her father understand. She was always falling in love with kittens, dogs, horses, it didn't matter. He would believe her. He never allowed Kate to keep the animals she wanted but at least he would understand her reasoning.

With the light from the garage highlighting his bald head, he nodded.

That was her cue to keep talking. He was allowing her the opportunity to explain before he made a decision.

"We named him Thunder." Kate was rambling. Her dad preferred direct and to-the-point communication. "The night before she planned to take him away we decided to hide him in the barn here at old...at Mr. Brown's." Kate heard Taylor gulp at the near slip at using old man Brown's nickname. "We thought we were making the right decision for Thunder."

Still no comment.

A flash of lightning lit up the sky in the far distance. Somewhere a dog barked.

Kate didn't want to say more but her father's silence bothered her. He *knew* it bothered her; that was the point.

"We tried to take care of him the best we could," Kate said, her voice quivering now. She didn't mean to almost cry but allowing the raw emotions to surface might actually help their case. Maybe her dad would understand.

"And you took it upon yourselves to hide the horse in someone else's barn?" he asked in a steady tone. That was his doctor's voice, being direct, to the point, while remaining calm. She admired his manner when he aimed it at someone else, but at the moment she felt as if she were under a microscope being analyzed.

"You made a dishonest choice, girls." Kate's dad rubbed his bald head, still highlighted by a streak of light flooding from the dusk-to-dawn lamp. "By not coming forth with your actions, and by keeping secrets, that's a form of lying. I believe you both know better."

The moms both nodded. Not so much as a noise escaped from them. Kate's mom usually voiced her opinion freely, but when Kate's dad was around, she let him do the talking. In this case, Kate preferred to hear one of her mother's lectures about disrespectful behavior than to hear her father's true words about lying and dishonesty. He was right. Kate had known the truth all along. She wished she had followed her gut instinct instead of agreeing to the crazy plan. But she had decided to make bad choices for the sake of keeping peace, and friends, at school. What a dumb idea.

Taylor was always good at reading Kate's thoughts. "Sir, it's not really Kate's fault. She tried to convince us not to hide Thunder, but she went along with it because we pressured her into helping us."

Kate's dad shook his head, rejecting the comment as fast as the words escaped Taylor's mouth. "Kate still went along with the plan. She didn't tell an adult, and she's out here in the middle of the night during a storm. She's responsible just as you are." Then he sharpened his stare at Taylor. "Who else is involved?"

Taylor pinched her lips closed.

If Taylor revealed the name of the other girls, she'd be called "Traitor Taylor" at school tomorrow, for sure. Or something worse. Lacey and Sarah would convince the popular girls to name call and poke fun at her. The pressures of being a girl!

"Out with it," Kate's dad said, narrowing his eyes. He glanced between Kate and Taylor with the full expectation that one of them confess.

If the pressure wasn't on before, it definitely was now. Kate had to fight to swallow, her throat feeling as though someone had his hands around her neck, trying to choke her. She hated all the lying, all the secrets. She wanted to return to the simple life she had known before she had met Thunder. Just thinking about him made her heart ache. They needed to find him.

"Sarah. Lacey." Taylor's voice sounded different, the pitch higher.

Kate's dad had no idea what school would be like tomorrow, or barn life for that matter.

Luckily her father had no clue whom the other girls were, but their mothers knew. Taylor's mom spoke up for the first time. "Lacey is the girl you've been hanging around lately," she said, more as a statement than a question.

Taylor shrugged off the comment.

"Taylor," her mom warned.

"I wouldn't say it was by choice," Taylor explained. "They sort of clung to us."

That wasn't the way it happened exactly. "Lacey fell in love with Thunder and claimed him as her own," Kate explained. "Then they tried to take over the Horse Club."

Kate's dad stood taller. He wasn't one for idle chitchat. "We need to let Mr. Brown get some sleep. We can talk about this somewhere else." He put his hand on Kate's shoulder and guided her toward the car. She climbed into the back seat, trying to keep as much distance from her dad as possible, and watched Taylor as she climbed into her own car, sitting in the front next to her mom. Brave Taylor. The adults talked for a brief moment, no doubt making a plan.

When Kate's dad slid behind the steering wheel in the driver's seat, he closed the door with a quiet but deafening click. He was too calm.

He pulled the car out of the driveway. Kate's mom followed in her own car but made a left turn instead of going right. Where was her dad headed?

He remained silent as he turned left onto another street, then right, and another left into the barn. *The barn.*

The lights were on in the bottom barn where Thunder's original stall was. Activity buzzed down there. Even though Kate strained to see out of the wet car window, she wasn't able to make out what was happening. There were two other cars in the parking lot, one Kate didn't recognize, and one that belonged to Layne. Why was Layne at the barn this late?

Kate swallowed hard.

As soon as her father parked, Kate swung her car door open.

"Before you get out," her dad said, "I want you to know that I understand why you hid the horse."

Kate gasped. "You do?"

"I get it, but the way you went about it was wrong. You can't give in to peer pressure, Kate." He opened his own door. "Life has a way of testing you. Be a leader, not a follower. You knew it was wrong to hide him. I understand how hard it is to do the right thing sometimes, but you have to trust your instincts, even when people are pushing you around. Take a stand, do the right thing."

She sat there in stunned silence. He understood her situation.

"That doesn't mean you won't get grounded, but you should know I understand." He climbed from the car. "Come on. Let's see if the horse returned here."

Kate climbed from the car and followed her father. Taylor's vehicle pulled in the parking lot but Kate didn't wait for her. Instead she stayed with her dad. Her friend would catch up soon enough and *together* they would deal with this mess.

CHAPTER TWENTY-FOUR

Kate slowed when Taylor jogged up behind her, falling into step with Kate's pace. As they neared the barn, Kate saw Layne close a stall door. There was a tall lady standing outside the stall that Kate didn't recognize.

"Who is that?" Taylor whispered.

"I don't know." Kate had a bad feeling.

As they approached, Layne glanced up at them. "Oh, good. These are the girls you need to meet," Layne said to the stranger. "Taylor and Kate. They've taken care of Thunder all this time."

A knot formed in Kate's belly.

The lady reached out her hand. "Thanks for caring for Brownie."

Who the heck was Brownie, and who the heck was she?

"Brownie is Thunder's real name. This is his owner," Layne explained.

Kate swore she stopped breathing for a brief

second or two. Owner?

Kate and Taylor exchanged looks.

Thunder stared out of the stall at the girls. Kate thought he looked guilty for jumping the fence and running away.

"I'm Mr. Patrick," Kate's dad said, extending his hand. He introduced the woman to Kate's mom, who joined them along with Taylor's mom.

"And I'm Mrs. Gibbons," Taylor's mom said.

"It's nice to meet everyone. I'm Miss Della." Miss Della had curly brown hair with highlights of silver running through it and cut just above her shoulder. She tucked a strand of curls behind her ear. "I've been looking for Brownie. He jumped over my paddock fence on a stormy night much like this one. He's afraid of storms and loud noises."

She wasn't saying anything Kate and Taylor hadn't learned. Be nice, Kate reminded herself.

Miss Della owned Brownie. How horrible. Could this night get any worse?

"How did you find him?" Taylor asked, her voice soft. The sad expression on her face gave away that she didn't want to know the truth anymore than Kate did. But then again, they were both naturally curious.

"I heard through another trainer that Layne had found a horse. I contacted her a couple of days ago, but she said the horse was missing."

Guilt crept into Kate's consciousness. In her

peripheral vision, she saw her dad staring at her. She avoided eye contact with him. They had kept the woman, Miss Della, from reclaiming her horse.

As if to inject humor in the situation, Thunder began flapping his lips together. Everyone laughed. Kate would miss him. She crossed behind the woman and stuck her hand between the bars to scratch Thunder on the nose. They would never see him again.

"I looked everywhere, called everyone I knew, but no one had any information on Brownie," Miss Della explained. "I started calling local trainers and that's how I discovered Layne had found a horse."

Despite Kate's reluctance to like the woman, she seemed sincere.

Kate turned her attention away from Thunder long enough to study Miss Della in more detail. She wore a long denim skirt with a bright flowered top and had on pink short boots to match the color of a few flowers in the shirt. The woman was a hippie. She wore no makeup, but to be fair, who wore makeup this time of night? The dim lighting didn't help, either. Who knew what she looked like outside in broad daylight, not that Kate had the right to judge the woman. The important thing was that Thunder belonged to her. Miss Della could call him Brownie all she wanted but he would always be Thunder to her.

"Where do you live?" Taylor asked.

Kate thanked Taylor silently for being the more outspoken one. Kate wanted to know the answers to the several questions dancing around in her mind, but the words refused to part her lips.

"I live off of Deer Park Road a few miles from here."

Deer Park Road. Why did that name sound so familiar?

"I have a small goat farm. Brownie is my *only* horse," she said.

Goat farm. Deer Park Road.

Kate racked her brain to remember. She had either heard something about a small goat farm, or she'd noticed the place when one of her parent's drove her to a friend's house off that road. The uneasy feeling grew. What did she know about that place?

"Can we come see him sometime?" Taylor asked.

"Taylor, that's too forward," her mother said with a pointed look.

"It's fine," Miss Della said. "I'd love the company. Sometimes Brownie gets lonely. His best friends are goats."

His *only* friends were goats. Something about Miss Della seemed familiar. Who was she?

Miss Della continued to ramble. "Just come by the house anytime. No need to call first. I'm usually home. And if I'm not, make yourself comfortable in the barn. Feel free to brush him and visit. Just don't ride him. He hasn't been ridden in about two years."

Kate held back a gasp.

"A girl used to show him before I bought him," Miss Della continued as she untucked the curl behind her ear. "He was recovering from an injury but he's healed completely now. It's hard to imagine I've had him for two years. He needs to be ridden again."

"Two years," Kate repeated. The words escaped her mouth. She clamped her hand over her lips to stop talking before she revealed too much information. Her father stared at her again, as if he knew the girls had ridden Thunder. Lacey was lucky he hadn't bucked her off.

Thunder stuck his nose up to the bars and nudged Kate's hand.

"He likes you," Miss Della remarked. "Of course, he's friendly with most people, but I can tell he has a special bond with you."

"Thank you," Kate said politely. "I like him too. But he really had a strong bond with a friend of ours. Her name is Lacey." Did she really just call Lacey a friend? What had come over her? That would be a short-lived friendship once her parents found out about Lacey's involvement in the situation.

Thunder wiggled his nose because Kate, lost in thought, stopped rubbing it. Kate giggled. "You're a ham."

"That he is," Miss Della said. "Layne called me tonight once Brownie returned to the barn. I have no idea where he's been, but I'm glad he's back."

Layne narrowed her brows and alternated an accusing glare between Kate and Taylor. She would corner them tomorrow when she had them alone at the barn. That was, if they were ever allowed to return to the barn. Kate was sure their parents would ground them for life and from everything they loved.

"Why don't you come by next week and check on him," Miss Della said, extending a generous offer.

"We'd love to," Kate said. She avoided glancing at her parents because they'd likely shake their heads in disagreement.

"Perfect. How about next weekend?" Miss Della asked. "Even a weekday is fine," she added.

Was the woman always so friendly, or was she lonely and in desperate need of company? Kate was grateful that Miss Della was warm and friendly, but at the same time Kate was cautious about visiting her. The woman loved to talk too much. That would get on Kate's nerves soon enough, but chatter got on Taylor's nerves even faster.

Next weekend sounded forever away because she was used to seeing Thunder daily, but chances were, Kate and Taylor would be grounded.

"And bring your friend, Lacey. I'm sure Brownie would enjoy seeing her again." The woman talked faster than Kate could think. "Maybe you girls could help me by riding him again."

Kate and Taylor exchanged another look that didn't go unnoticed by Kate's perceptive father. She wasn't about to admit that Lacey had already mounted him. They were in enough trouble as it was.

"We'll see about the riding part," Layne said. "In the meantime, say your goodbyes to the horse. He's leaving first thing in the morning while you both are in school."

A well of emotion surfaced with surprising force from a deep place in Kate's heart. She bit back tears. No way was she ready to bid Thunder farewell. And once Lacey realized he'd left without a chance for her to say goodbye, she'd be more than upset. Sure, Miss Della said they could visit, but it was possible that was an empty promise. People said things like that all the time.

Kate refused to allow herself to cry.

Taylor broke the awkward silence that followed by opening Thunder's stall door. She wrapped her ropey arms around his slender neck, holding onto him with force. Her friend buried her face deep into his neck.

Oh, gosh. Don't look. Kate turned her head before she broke into a raging waterfall of tears. Her throat burned from unshed tears. She hadn't realized how much she'd grown to love the animal.

Taylor's mom stepped into the stall behind her daughter and offered her hand for support on Taylor's shoulder. Kate hoped her own parents didn't touch her, because if they did, she'd lose it. The last thing she wanted was to cry in front of all these people, especially Layne. Kate tried so hard to appear tough in front of her trainer.

"It's all right, Taylor," her mother said. "I promise I'll take you girls to see him."

Thunder acted as though he understood what was going on. He lowered his head, wrapped his neck around Taylor, and nuzzled her leg. It appeared he was hugging her back.

Miss Della stayed where she was but said, "I promise you can come to see him anytime you wish." The woman wiped her own eyes.

That was it. Kate ran from the barn. As soon as she was in the safety of a darkened corner of the parking lot, out of reach of the floodlights, the tears streamed down her cheeks. She jumped when someone touched the small of her back. It was her father.

"I promise too," he said in that quiet, calm voice. This time, though, the voice wasn't aimed at comforting a patient, but directed at her.

His words, his touch, warmed her heart. He was a man of honor. Grounded or not, he'd see to it that the girls visited Thunder. She assumed that included Lacey. How were they supposed to break the news to her?

CHAPTER TWENTY-FIVE

All morning long Kate avoided Lacey at school, but then they had science class together and lunch. They never sat with each other in the lunch room, but today of all days, Lacey and Sarah chose to sit across from them at their table.

Taylor was good at facing difficult topics head-on. Maybe she'd break the news to them. They hadn't talked to the girls since their argument at old man Brown's barn. Why now?

Lacey edged closer to Kate, sitting directly across from her and ignoring Taylor all together. Kate figured that was most likely because of the verbal disagreement the two of them exchanged the last time they had seen each other.

"I was thinking about riding Thunder after school today," Lacey said. "Want to meet at the barn?"

Kate swallowed hard. Come on, Taylor. Tell her!

Taylor continued to pull the crust off her peanut butter sandwich. She made no attempt to explain anything.

"Well?" Lacey pushed for an answer.

"About that..." Apparently, Kate was on her own to explain the details concerning Thunder.

At Kate's hesitance, Lacey's eyebrows raised in question. "Are you seriously still mad at me? I need to see Thunder."

Kate wanted to crawl under the table. "You can see him."

Lacey's eyebrows scrunched together and her mouth drew into a deep frown. "What's the problem then?"

"He's not at old man Brown's barn anymore," Taylor said, clearly enjoying taunting Lacey.

"What's that supposed to mean?" Lacey's voice rose enough that a teacher asked them to quiet down. She lowered her voice, but the tone was sharp enough to almost cut someone.

Before Kate answered, Taylor smiled. "He's gone, as in he's been moved."

Lacey scooted down the bench in front of Taylor. She leaned across the table until she was barely a foot away from Taylor's face. "I want answers now," Lacey growled. "What are you hiding from me?"

Kate leaned closer to them, so no one would overhear. "He escaped last night during the storm.

The thunder spooked him and he jumped the paddock fence." Not that she owed Lacey an answer, but she wanted to keep the peace between them instead of agitating her more as Taylor was so enjoying. "Layne found his owner and they are trailering him home today."

Lacey shot backward on the bench, putting distance between the girls. Her mouth had dropped open, her face pale enough that Kate thought she might throw up. Sarah sat there quietly absorbing the news.

"Gone?" The words squeaked out of Lacey's mouth.

"Yep. We met his owner last night," Taylor said, prolonging the enjoyment of annoying Lacey.

Kate interrupted again. "Miss Della owns him, and she mentioned we could visit anytime we'd like. She wanted to know if you'd help ride him."

"I already ride him," Lacey said. A smile spread across her face at the memory.

"He hasn't been ridden in two years." Taylor zipped closed her lunch bag with casual interest, as if what she said wasn't a surprise. "You're lucky he didn't throw you off."

Lacey had no smart-mouthed comeback.

"Yep, two years." Taylor stood and grabbed the trash off the table. She walked over to the trashcan and dumped the waste into the garbage. Without another word to Lacey, she grabbed hold of her lunch bag and sat with another group of girls.

The traitor. Her best friend left Kate to deal with the aftermath.

"Where does Thunder live?" Sarah asked, recovering first from the shock.

"Some goat farm on Deer Park road," Kate said. She wished she could move tables to join Taylor, but her butt remained planted on the bench.

"That's only a few miles from here," Sarah commented.

"A goat farm on Deer Park Road," Lacey repeated, then gasped. "That's the rundown place with the goats running all over. Someone said they even chew the siding off the house. The place isn't fit to live in."

Kate stopped eating and put down the remainder of the chips left in the bag.

"I remember that place," Sarah said too loud and the teacher shushed them again.

Now Kate understood why the goat farm stood out in her mind. The place was awful! She knew Miss Della's name sounded familiar, added to the fact she had a goat farm. She had heard a few girls at the barn talking about the rundown place. Kate shivered at the thought of Thunder living under those conditions. She wanted to hide him again, although she assumed she was supposed to have learned that lesson already.

Taylor glanced over but turned away before

Kate acknowledged her. If she wanted to know what they were discussing, then she needed to return to the seat she abandoned. Even without the support of her friend, Kate thought she was dealing with the situation quite well.

"What are we going to do to save him?" Sarah asked.

"No, you don't," Kate said. After all, she had in fact learned a valuable lesson. Be a leader, not a follower, her father had said. She wasn't about to be part of another crazy scheme, not to mention that Lacey and Sarah hadn't been around to carry the weight when the adults found out about Thunder. They had left Kate and Taylor to take the heat. "Let the authorities handle it."

Lacey snickered. "You are so naïve, Kate. What are the cops going to do? They can't remove a horse because the place is a mess."

"Neither can you," Kate said. "It was one thing to steal him from our barn, but it's another thing to steal him from his owner's home. It doesn't matter if you agree with the way she cares for him or not. It's not your business."

A nearby girl stared at them. To Kate's knowledge, no one ever stood up to the popular Lacey. Well, it was about time someone did. Too bad Taylor wasn't within earshot so she could appreciate the confrontation.

To Kate's surprise, Lacey backed off. Was that

all it took to make a bully stop? Again, the word confidence popped into Kate's mind. It wasn't about the words she chose to use but about the calm, confident tone, in which Kate delivered the message. She was more like her father than she thought. She copied the same tone he used, and no one dared bully him. She fought back a giggle at the image of anyone attempting such a task.

Kate needed to keep the upper hand. She stood, gathered her belongings, and left the table. Taylor made room on the bench next to her.

"People are staring at you," Taylor whispered.

"That's because I stood up to Lacey."

Taylor nodded in approval. "I heard part of it. You let her have an earful."

Kate hadn't been aware that she'd spoken loud enough for other people to hear.

"Even the teacher didn't stop you. It has been a long time coming," Taylor said. "I bet she was cheering you on."

Kate's confidence grew more. She hadn't set out to accomplish putting Lacey in her place. Maybe that was another reason Lacey backed off. It was honest, to the point, calm, and said in a don't-mess-with-me tone. Her father's tone, for sure.

Lunch was over. Kids stood up in chaos, throwing away trash, shuffling toward the doorway, and taking a moment to stare at Kate without speaking. Kate wasn't sure if their reaction was one of respect, or one of protecting Lacey. Time would tell.

The day went by faster than Kate wanted. While the kids at school gaped at her the rest of the day, there was a worse force to deal with once her father returned home from the office. She would find out tonight about her punishment.

CHAPTER TWENTY-SIX

"Jump the outside line," Layne told Kate. "Make sure you ride your corners."

Kate listened as best she could. Corners were never her strong suit. She always wanted to cut them short instead of lining up Razor for a better takeoff spot before they reached the jump. He was an amazing horse, but he needed more help from her than what she usually offered. Old habits were hard to break.

She steered him deeper into the corner, at least deep enough in her mind.

"Perfect! Stay right there and you have it," Layne said.

For the first time Kate saw their takeoff spot a few strides away. Razor jumped with flawless form as they sailed over the first jump. His strides afterward were flowing and easy. Maybe Kate needed to ride the corners deeper more often. The second jump was just as wonderful as the first one.

"Yes!" Layne said. Enthusiastic praise from her didn't come often. Kate's confidence in jumping soared to a new level. "You're finished. Now we need to talk."

Just because Kate and Taylor made it through the entire lesson without Layne bringing up the subject of Thunder, Kate knew Layne's lecture was coming. Kate realized her trainer was only doing her job, but any criticism from Layne was bothersome. Kate wanted to stay in her good graces, to stay in that joyful state she experienced just a moment ago when Layne praised her. Kate despised conflict, although lately conflict seemed to follow her everywhere.

"You know what you did wrong, so I'm not going to stress that point. Bottom line, you went behind my back and made me look unprofessional when Miss Della called looking for her horse. I had no idea where he was. What kind of barn do you think I run? In Miss Della's eyes, I failed as a trainer to know what was happening in my own barn."

Kate hadn't considered Layne in the situation. She had been focused on hiding things from her parents, pleasing her friends, and caring for Thunder. Kate thought she was being responsible, except the obvious part about removing Thunder from the barn, but she never thought about how their actions would impact Layne.

"I'm sorry, Layne." Kate meant the apology.

"Me too," Taylor said. They were walking their horses around the arena to cool them down. "I guess we got caught up in the moment of saving Thunder."

"I'm sure you meant well for the horse, but sometimes you have to look at the bigger picture." Layne sat down on the mounting block and looped her arms around her knees. "I don't expect you to understand this, but the horse world is difficult. You have to be as professional as possible to be successful. You both compromised that for me."

Kate understood what her trainer was saying, but the fact that Lacey and Sarah weren't here again to take responsibility bothered her. They were all in this together. Why was it that Kate and Taylor took the brunt of the confrontations from the adults for their crazy actions as a team? Her dad's words flooded her mind.

Stay true to your beliefs. If you follow friends when you know what they are doing is wrong, the punishment will always fall back on you, not them. That's the way it usually works out.

She thought about mentioning to Layne the involvement of the other girls, but that would only make Layne mad and appear that Kate was trying to escape responsibility. No, she had to suck it up this time.

"I never thought hiding Thunder would hurt

you," Kate said. "I'm truly sorry."

"Me too," Taylor added again. "Question, though. It seems Thunder is living in a run-down barn invaded with goats. We hate that for him. They say the house is neglected too."

Kate wanted to add that Lacey wanted to steal him away again but she didn't dare. Like she told Lacey today at lunch, it was none of their business.

Layne's mouth dropped open for a slight moment before she recovered, but Kate caught her surprise.

"Go visit him," Layne suggested. "If he's neglected we can call animal control. We have to let the law handle things even if we disagree with how he's being treated. Chances are, though, what you heard is a rumor. People have different thoughts about how to care for animals. At this barn we blanket our horses, spoil them rotten, but that doesn't mean a horse is neglected without those things."

She had a point. Kate hoped she was right, that it was a rumor. Thunder deserved the best care possible.

Later that night, when Kate's dad returned home, she was waiting for him in the kitchen. Instead of avoiding the conversation as she normally would, she wanted it to be over. Also, she planned to find out when she could visit Thunder. She needed to see for herself that Miss Della was taking good care of him.

Her father set down his brief case on the far counter. He poured a filtered glass of ice water from the refrigerator and offered Kate one. She declined, ready to head off this discussion.

First things first, she wanted to tell him about the confrontation with Lacey and everyone's reaction. "Dad, can I share what happened today at school?"

He stood at the counter, taking a long sip of water. When he set the glass down, he said, "Of course. You can always talk to me."

"I told Lacey about what happened last night, and that Thunder left with Miss Della today. Lacey was bullying us and Taylor walked away, but I sat there and addressed the issue. She mentioned that Miss Della has a rundown house and neglected barn. She thinks Thunder is in a bad situation there. She mentioned taking him again and hiding him from Miss Della."

He raised his eyebrows. "What did you say to her?"

Kate wished she'd accepted the glass of water he'd offered because her mouth went dry. She could barely swallow. "I told her to let the police handle the situation, that taking Thunder from our barn was bad enough, but to steal him from his owner was against the law. I told her it was none of our business."

A smile spread across his face. "Very good."

She waited for him to say more but he didn't.

"Thanks," Kate said. She didn't know why she had wanted to share the information with her dad. She guessed she wanted him to say something more. When he didn't, she couldn't help feeling disappointment.

"Twice now Taylor and I were left holding the bag. We got in trouble, and they didn't. That's not fair."

"I think you learned a valuable lesson," her dad said finally. "But instead of getting involved with Lacey's scheme to steal the horse again, you coached her to reach for a better solution. On top of that, you learned that certain types of people hang around for the adventure, but when it goes wrong, they disappear and leave you standing there dealing with what they created."

She knew he would say that, and he was right.

"As much as I am tempted to ground you, I have to ask myself what my goal is with punishment. What you learned was far more important than being grounded for any length of time. What more could a parent want?"

She hadn't predicted his reasonable response.

"So I'm not going to ground you."

Or that response, either. She inhaled a long, deep breath.

"Dad, I don't understand." Kate needed to stop

talking because he wasn't grounding her, but a wave of guilt replaced the temporary feeling of relief. Honestly? She deserved punishment.

"I want you to learn to think for yourself, to walk away when someone is engaging in wrong behavior." He patted her shoulder and his approval was reward enough. "You demonstrated that today, Kate. Good job."

Unbelievable. He was rewarding her for standing up to Lacey. Not only did she shock herself by the bold move, and most of the kids in the lunchroom, her father was proud of her too. Kate wondered if Taylor's parents would be as understanding.

"Thanks, dad." She loved pleasing him.

"As far as Thunder is concerned, I want to make sure he is safe and that his needs are being met," he said. "While his living arrangements are none of our business, it's obvious you and the other girls care for him. What would it hurt to visit?"

Kate sat up straighter. "When?"

"How about tomorrow? It's my early day off."

She hoped Taylor was free to go with her. If not, she could ask Lacey to join her, but under the circumstances, she would rather avoid Lacey altogether.

CHAPTER TWENTY-SEVEN

The next day at school was painful. Sam, dressed in
jeans and a bright blue polo shirt that matched his
gorgeous eyes, approached Kate in the lunchroom.
She hadn't talked to him since she had found out he
asked Lacey to the dance.

"Hi," he said with an awkward hitch in his
voice.

Kate tossed the remains from her lunch into the
trash can. She had no clue what to say to him, so
she nodded.

He didn't let the silence bother him. "What are
you doing this weekend? Maybe I could come
watch you ride."

Kate thought about accepting, but if he had in
fact asked Lacey to the dance, then she wanted
nothing to do with him. Although, to give him the
benefit of the doubt, she wasn't sure he'd actually
asked Lacey. It was possible the other girl lied.
Kate, feeling brave, looked him square in the eyes.

"Lacey mentioned you asked her to the dance. Is that true?"

His mouth dropped open, and when he recovered, he rolled his eyes. "Kate, she asked me to the dance. I didn't ask her."

"How did you answer?"

"She caught me off guard, so I told her I'd think about it." He reached out and touched Kate's elbow. "I don't want to go with her. I want to take you."

Confused, Kate stood still without pulling away from his touch. "But you didn't tell her no."

"I didn't tell her yes," he reasoned. "And I never brought up the subject again."

Kate wasn't sure why but his lack of declining Lacey's offer bothered her. "That's not good enough," she said. Either he wanted to take Lacey or he didn't. It was a yes or no answer.

Lacey walked by them and watched closely. Was she jealous that Sam was talking to her?

Sam took that opportunity to clear up the misunderstanding. He flagged over Lacey. When she approached, Lacey chose to stand closer to Sam than to Kate. Their arms were touching. Sam let go of Kate's elbow. "You asked me to the dance," he said, directly addressing the situation. "I can't go because I asked Kate to the dance. I hope she says yes because I want to go with her."

Kate stood there with her mouth gaped open.

Did guys really say things like that? About her? He wanted to take *her* to the dance, and he was making things right with Kate as a witness. Unbelievable.

Lacey's face hardened. Without a word she stomped away, almost knocking Kate over from the angry bump as their shoulders met.

After Lacey disappeared in the safety net of her gossiping friends, Sam asked Kate to the dance again. "I'd love to go with you," Kate said. Her mind twirled in circles from the change of events.

His wide smile almost melted Kate's heart into a puddle next to her feet. Taylor would suggest that Kate not let Sam know how much she liked him, but at that moment Kate didn't think she could hide the smile forming on her own face.

"Can I watch you ride this weekend?" he asked again.

"Yes." He was more than welcome to watch her anytime he wanted. They both loved the same sport. "I can ask Layne if you can exercise one of her horses. We can ride together."

"Okay," he said before taking Kate's empty lunch tray from her. Even the way he stacked it atop the others was adorable. Oh, she had it bad. Or good. Whatever.

After school ended, Kate's dad picked them up from car line. Waiting all day to see Thunder was difficult to say the least. Taylor came back to Kate's house to change clothes and grab a snack.

"I hope you don't mind," Taylor said, "but I asked Lacey to meet us at Miss Della's farm to see Thunder."

A small growl escaped Kate's throat. "What?" Kate couldn't believe her ears. "You asked the enemy to go with us without running it by me first?"

"What's wrong with you?" Taylor asked.

"Are you kidding? Lacey asked Sam to the dance, not the other way around. It almost broke us up."

"If he wants to go with her, then he doesn't deserve you."

"That's true, but he wants to go with me." Kate rubbed her forehead to ward off a headache. Life was such drama. "He asked me to the dance in front of Lacey and she got mad. We aren't talking."

Taylor swallowed the last bite of a chocolate-chip cookie and drank the last gulp of milk in her glass before she set it on the counter. She let out an exaggerated "Ahhh" before standing, ready to leave. "If she doesn't talk to you, then what are you complaining about?"

"Don't dismiss this," Kate said, standing up against her friend for once.

"You have the upper hand," Taylor said. "Your dad arranged this meeting with Miss Della, and Lacey is joining us. If Lacey wants to behave like a jerk, no sweat off our backs."

"Correction. No sweat off your back," Kate said.

"Besides, she's our best chance of getting better care for Thunder," Taylor said, ignoring Kate's comment.

"How so?"

"Lacey has a special bond with him. Maybe Miss Della will recognize that and let us come around more. That will allow us to make sure he is well taken care of."

Taylor was always so smart.

Kate's dad walked into the kitchen. "Ready?"

"We are," Kate said, rinsing the small cookie plate and placing it along with the two milk glasses into the dishwasher. When finished the girls followed him into the garage.

"We're picking up Lacey," he said before they reached the car. "Her parents called and asked if she could ride with us."

Kate groaned. Taylor noticed, flashing her a warning look not to mess up the plan. Kate glared back. Couldn't she enjoy life without Lacey always ruining things?

They climbed into the car. Kate had to make a special effort not to slam the car door. If she had, her father would not appreciate the outburst. Before long, they pulled into Lacey's driveway and, because her father's laptop and a stack of files covered the front seat, the girl slithered into the backseat with Taylor sandwiched between them. Having the girl in the car made the confined space even tighter, stuffy with tension. Kate needed space from the bully. Kate's dad would remind her that bullies were people too, and that there was a reason they behaved in a less than desirable way.

Their behavior says something about them, Kate. Don't take it personally. He was always right. Kate needed to remember his words.

Thank goodness the drive was short. As they pulled up the long driveway, Kate gasped. Poor Thunder.

The fences were broken, mended by duct tape in places. Some of the paddocks had only electric fencing containing the animals, but the wire was lying on the ground in various spots, so the fences were useless. Goats darted around the bare pasture and chickens ran free. The barn was unpainted with several boards falling off the building with one end resting on the ground.

"Oh, Dad," Kate said staring out the window.

"It's rough, honey," he said. "Try to look for positives. We can't change the situation but we can attempt to improve it."

A quiet sob sounded from Lacey. Thunder's dire situation touched Lacey's heartstrings.

Even though Kate was mad at the girl, she tried to offer support. "I'm sorry, Lacey. Like my dad said, we'll try to help him. We've cleaned up old man Brown's barn; we can clean up this one."

Lacey wiped a streak off her cheek and nodded.

Kate's dad pulled into a tight spot near the barn. A whinny called out from the nearest stall window. Kate smiled when she saw Thunder's nose touching the stall bars of the window. How he knew who was visiting was beyond Kate.

"He knows it's us," Lacey said in a small voice. She opened the car door and bounded out.

Kate and Taylor darted into the barn. Thunder whinnied when he saw them and met the girls at the stall door. Lacey didn't wait for Miss Della to join them before she opened the stall door and wrapped her arms around Thunder's long, slender neck. Kate wasn't sure, but she imagined that more tears streamed down Lacey's face. Despite her anger toward the girl, the scene touched Kate. She found herself almost liking Lacey. When she was vulnerable, she didn't seem like such a bully. Maybe her dad was right. Bullies are people too. Lacey's poor behavior was caused by some unknown reason to Kate. Was Lacey worth the effort to figure out the reason?

Miss Della and Kate's father joined them in the barn. Her father walked up behind Kate and touched her elbow. His kind touch nearly sent Kate into tears too.

"He's glad to see you, my dear." Miss Della wore a bright-colored, tie-die sun dress. She had her

wild hair pulled back to one side. It was obvious to
Kate that the woman was a free spirit, whatever that
meant. Her mom used that word to describe a
person who was carefree, artsy, creative, and
embraced life in a way that didn't allow rules to
limit them. If Kate tried to be free spirited, her
parents and teachers would stop her before she
started. A little giggle escaped Kate but no one
seemed to notice.

"You can take him out of the stall," Miss Della
told Lacey.

Lacey's face was wet with tears. She wasn't
able to speak but forced a little smile on her lips in
silent answer to Miss Della. Taylor handed Lacey a
halter that was hanging from a rusty hook outside
the stall door.

Lacey held the halter out to Thunder and he
lowered his head to place his muzzle in the
noseband. She hooked the halter on him. The others
cleared a path for Lacey to lead him out of the dirty
stall.

One way the girls could help was to start with
cleaning out his stall. Kate wanted to scrub his
water buckets, refill them with fresh water, and put
new shavings in the stall. She glanced around and
saw a small pile of shavings in the far corner. At
least the pile was inside the barn for protection from
rainy weather. Maybe she could talk her dad into
buying a large load. That way, if they visited after

school often, they had shavings to clean his stall. It appeared that Miss Della couldn't afford shavings, so if she had a pile handy, maybe she'd be more inclined to keep the stall clean. Kate busied herself with shoveling manure. It took several trips to the compost pile outside, but she would sleep well tonight knowing his stall was clean.

There were no crossties in the aisle, so Taylor held Thunder's lead rope while Lacey cleaned him with a couple of brushes stored in a small purple bucket supplied by Miss Della. The brushes were caked with mud—another thing the girls could help with. Kate wanted to wash the brushes; Thunder deserved the best. Lacey made do with what she had and removed the caked-on mud from Thunder's coat. By the time she finished, he had a slight shine to him.

"He looks gorgeous," Kate said, impressed.

Miss Della beamed. "He does. And I can tell he really loves you, Lacey."

Lacey swallowed hard. She was probably fighting off tears again. She didn't answer but turned toward Thunder and rubbed his forehead. It was obvious to Kate that the girl, who Kate was starting to like despite her strong negative side, was having a difficult time dealing with her emotions.

An hour or so slipped by so fast Kate was surprised when her father glanced at his watch. She knew that meant he was ready to leave.

Disappointed at having to say goodbye already, Kate made a point to wrap up things with her friends to save her father from having to speak up.

Lacey walked Thunder back to his fresh clean stall. His water buckets were clean enough for the girls to almost drink from them. Kate had used most of the shavings from the pile to fill Thunder's stall but saved enough so Miss Della had enough for tomorrow. Lacey slid the stall door closed as if she were saying goodbye to him forever. She hung up his halter on the hook with care.

"Do you want to ride him next time?" Miss Della asked Lacey.

Lacey's head snapped up as she faced Miss Della. "I'd love that." Her voice sounded thick from unexpressed sorrow.

"When can we come back?" Kate asked her dad. Why was she helping Lacey so much? That was when Kate realized helping out was for her as much as it was for Thunder and Lacey.

Lacey inhaled a deep breath. She seemed to appreciate Kate's help with organizing their next visit. Kate knew Lacey's parents weren't as supportive as Kate's, and if they wanted to visit Thunder again, they had to rely on Kate's parents to drive. Taylor's mom had her hands full with the twins.

"Thursday. Come out after school and you can ride," Miss Della said.

After school was difficult, and Tuesdays were the days Kate's father left the office early. She wasn't sure how ideal Thursday was. She glanced at her dad, silently asking him for permission.

"That's fine," her dad said. Kate knew his answer meant he would figure out how to get them there. His word was solid.

"We'll see you then," Miss Della said as she gave Lacey a hug. "I must tell you, Thunder hasn't been ridden in a long while. We'll have to start slowly."

A smile smile flashed ever so briefly across Lacey's lips. "I can handle it," she said. Not that the adults realized, thank goodness, but the girls already knew Lacey rode him well. How would Lacey pull of pretending to ride him for the first time?

CHAPTER TWENTY-EIGHT

The following night the Horse Club girls were almost finished with their horses in the barn when a thunderstorm arrived from nowhere. The sky grew dark and lightning lit up the entrance to the barn.

"I have homework and need to get home," Taylor said, studying the sky from a safe distance inside the barn.

"Me too," Kate said. The downpour covered the asphalt parking lot. "I'm not about to run to my mom's car in this storm." She had to yell over the loud pounding from the rain on the tin roof.

Lacey and Sarah had already finished with their horses and had put them back in their stalls. Lacey leaned against the stall door of the schooling horse she rode tonight, watching him munch on hay. Sarah sat on a nearby tack trunk in the aisle to wait out the storm.

"They should outlaw homework," Taylor continued to complain. "I mean…we work all day at school. Evenings are for my horse."

Lightning lit up the aisle. A clap of thunder boomed overhead, causing Kate to jump. The rumble rattled her soul. She loved a good thunderstorm if safe at home, but at the barn the lightning unnerved her. Another flash, another boom. The storm seemed to last forever.

A whinny sounded from the parking lot. A moment later a dark horse galloped into the entrance of the barn and skidded to a stop. He snorted from fear.

Thunder!

He stood with his forelegs wide apart as if wanting to run off. Another snort filled the night.

Lacey popped up from leaning against the stall door. Thunder jumped in place and Kate thought he was thinking about an escape plan. He didn't like the storm raging behind him, but the girls were in front of him. He didn't have a place to run. Lacey stepped forward with caution.

"It's okay, boy." Lacey held out her hand to let him sniff. He snorted instead. "You're okay."

He lowered his head somewhat. He was starting to relax until another boom of thunder cracked overhead. He scooted forward, almost bumping into Lacey.

"Taylor, can you hand me a halter?" Lacey asked.

Taylor pulled a halter off one of the doors and

walked slowly, as not to spook Thunder, and handed the halter to Lacey.

"Whoa, baby." Lacey reached out her hand again. This time Thunder sniffed it. She held out the halter as she had done many times before. As usual, Thunder placed his nose into the nose band and allowed Lacey to fasten the strap.

"Well, this time we know who owns him," Kate said. Razor, who was edgy from all the action, paced back and forth in the crossties. Kate unhooked her horse and returned him to his stall. As soon as she removed the halter, he turned on his haunches to dive bomb the hay.

When Kate returned to the aisle, Lacey was holding Thunder, rubbing his face and between his ears. He was more relaxed, his head lowered, and the snorting had stopped. The result was one relaxed horse even during the raging storm. Bottom line, he trusted Lacey.

"What are we going to do with him?" Kate asked. She had learned an important lesson the last time around.

"Call Miss Della," Taylor suggested.

Surprised at Taylor's answer, Kate let out a long breath.

"We can't do that," Lacey said. "Miss Della's place is horrible."

Not wanting to get caught up in Lacey's irrational emotions anymore, Kate squared her shoulders to the other girl. Bully or not, Kate had enough of Lacey pushing her around. "No, we are calling Miss Della. If there's one thing I learned, it's to be honest and not to hide someone else's horse. Taylor and I were punished for the last adventure. I don't plan to revisit that."

Lacey stared at Kate as if she were a foreign object.

"If you decide to hide Thunder, I'm out." No matter what, Kate planned to stand her ground.

"I'm out too," Taylor said, siding with Kate. There was power in two people sticking together.

Sarah didn't speak. Perhaps she was afraid to go against her friend's wishes. Whatever.

"You'll tell if I hide him," Lacey said.

Kate didn't deny the truth and nodded. Yes, she'd tell her father the truth. No way was she going to support Lacey's crazy idea again.

The silence made Lacey squirm. "Fine. We'll call Miss Della," she said with reluctance thick in her voice.

"Actually, my suggestion is to call Layne and let her deal with Miss Della," Taylor said. "That removes us from the situation."

Sarah remained quiet. Didn't she have an opinion?

"I second that thought," Kate said.

"Can we wait until morning?" Lacey asked.

The thought of Lacey asking permission from

them was bittersweet. How things had changed for the better. She was listening, taking direction from them.

"We'll be in school tomorrow," Kate reasoned. "If we call Layne tonight, she can call Miss Della before it gets late."

Lacey snuggled into Thunder's neck. Kate almost felt sorry for the girl. She needed a horse to love, one of her own, like the rest of them.

"You're right," Lacey said. "But I can't do it. Will you, Kate? I mean, will you call Layne tonight for me?"

Again, Lacey surprised Kate. "Of course. I'd be happy to help you out."

Lacey kept the side of her face against Thunder's neck. He didn't seem to mind. "That's what friends are for, and I appreciate it."

Friends? Lacey thought of them as friends?

"No worries," Kate said, even though her heart was racing from what Lacey had said. "I'll tell Layne tonight."

"Tell me what?" Layne asked as she entered the barn. She stopped in place when she saw Thunder.

"Thunder returned. Can you call Miss Della?" Kate was taking her rare role as the leader seriously. She was feeling confident and proud of herself for standing up against Lacey and speaking her mind. And it hadn't been that tough to say no. Kate must have spoken to Lacey with confidence, causing the other girl to trust her enough to listen.

Layne ran her hand over Thunder, making sure he hadn't gotten hurt in his haste to leave home and the storm behind. "I'll give her a call. I'm sure Miss Della will come get him tomorrow, so you might want to say goodbye tonight."

As if Thunder understood Layne's words, he tossed his head in argument.

"He doesn't want to go home," Lacey said.

"But he has no choice," Layne reminded them. "Someone else owns him."

Thunder lowered his head, rubbing his face into Lacey. Her cheeks were wet with tears again.

"I'm sorry, Lacey." Layne placed her hand on top of Lacey's head. "If you want a horse we'll find you one. There are tons of them for sale."

"But she wants Thunder," Kate said, surprised she was standing up for Lacey after all the aggravation she had caused her.

"I can ask if she'd sell him, but I doubt it. Are you interested?"

"My parents can't afford to buy a horse. They might agree to a free one," Lacey said.

"Of course, there is the price of board, which is inexpensive in comparison because you live in an equestrian neighborhood, but you'll still have veterinarian bills, and farrier work," Layne explained.

"I'll ask my parents but unless he's free, there's no way," Lacey said.

"We can try to earn the money," Kate said. Why was she helping the girl?

"With his prior show record, I'm sure he wouldn't be cheap. Although he hasn't been ridden in a while, so that helps keep his price down," Layne said. "He had an injury at one time so his price will be lower because of that too."

"But a lower price is not free," Kate said, protecting Lacey again.

"That's true," Layne said. "There is no way Miss Della will give him away. It's my understanding she needs money."

"I understand," Lacey said, more tears trickling down her face. "When the time is right I'll get a horse. Until then, I'll keep taking lessons." again."

CHAPTER TWENTY-NINE

The next day at school Kate noticed that Lacey was having a difficult time. Her eyes were red and puffy. Kate wouldn't be surprised if the girl was awake most of the night crying about Thunder. For sure, the horse returning to the barn stirred up emotions and memories of the first night he arrived in Lacey's life. Without a doubt, she was in love with the horse.

Kate appreciated owning Razor even more. While her parents had bought her a wonderful horse, a Christmas present nonetheless, Kate had to admit, she'd had a hard time leasing her pony out to little Candice. The agreement had been for Kate to keep both horses. Kate was blessed. She had two horses while Lacey had none.

Lacey sat down next to Kate again in the lunch room. When the popular girls joined them, including Kate in some of their chatter, Kate's mind whirled. It was one thing to get along better with

Lacey, and Kate had always thought being with the popular girls was an awesome idea, but it was another thought to sit with them at lunch. People were staring at her. Were they impressed or just surprised that the popular girls were talking to her? Kate had to admit she wasn't enjoying the attention as she had once thought. She was actually a bit uncomfortable. She viewed herself as a normal girl, with genuine friends. The popular group talked about boys, makeup, and the upcoming dance. Kate's friends talked about horses, going to the barn, and the latest test in math class. If they talked about boys, it was innocent and brief.

Kate longed for her friends to sit down next to her but they sat at another table. They left her to tolerate the popular girls on her own. Did they think she had betrayed them by joining forces with the girls who usually teased them?

Lacey turned to Kate. "Can I have one of your pretzels?"

Kate pushed the bag toward her.

"Thanks for understanding about Thunder. You helped me out and I appreciate it."

"I'm sure it's not easy to see him leave again," Kate said. She shoved a pretzel in her mouth.

"I wish Miss Della would give him to me."

An idea popped into Kate's mind. "Why don't you see if she'll give you a free lease. That way she still owns him but you can keep him at the barn and ride him whenever you want."

Lacey paused with her hand in Kate's pretzel bag. "Great idea. Think she'll do that?"

"Not sure," Kate replied. "She seems fond of her animals. I don't see her letting him go, but it's worth asking. If not, you can still ride him."

"It's not the same. I'd love to ride him with my friends." Lacey shoved the pretzel into her mouth. She chewed while she talked. "It's hard to get someone to drive me to Miss Della's. If Thunder stayed at our barn I could walk there whenever I wanted."

"True. At least my parents drive us once in a while, like tomorrow. Glad you'll get to ride him." Kate wanted to pull her bag of remaining pretzels closer to her so Lacey would stop eating them but she resisted the urge. "Maybe if Miss Della sees how well he does for you, she'll be impressed and want you to ride Thunder often. It's a win-win situation. She gets free training and you get to ride."

Lacey grabbed the last pretzel and Kate fought irritation. What nerve. Kate would never take the last pretzel from someone's lunch. Did Lacey think because she was popular she didn't have to be respectful, or was she just clueless?

"You're right," Lacey admitted. "It's a winning combination for both of us. Guess I can't have everything I want."

The next day after school, Kate's mom drove

Lisa Morgan

them to Miss Della's house. Thunder was back in a
dirty stall. Kate's parents had had a load of shavings
delivered this morning but Miss Della hadn't
cleaned the filthy stall yet. Kate's heart went out to
the horse. He deserved so much better. As her dad
said, it wasn't their business. Kate wanted to make
it their business, but if they caused trouble, Miss
Della would take away visiting rights. They had to
choose their battles.

While Lacey tacked up Thunder to ride, Kate
and Taylor cleaned his stall. It wasn't as bad as
she'd thought—they had cleaned it a couple of days
earlier—but the center spot was soiled with urine.
Thunder had mixed the manure in with the
shavings, probably due to his nerves during the
storm, so they had to clean the entire stall again.

"How do you think Thunder escaped the stall
during the storm?" Kate asked Taylor.

She glanced around. "I bet his stall door wasn't
locked all the way, or maybe she had him out in the
paddock. We know he likes to jump fences."

Kate stood on her toes to look out the small
window in his stall. "There is a paddock with the
top fence board half off. He could jump that easily."

"Why would she have him outside in a storm
with no shelter?" Taylor asked.

Kate shrugged. "The storm came on suddenly."

Lacey led Thunder out of the barn.

"Let's watch her ride to make sure she's safe.

He hasn't been ridden much," Kate said.

"Why are you always looking out for Lacey? I thought you didn't like her?"

"That's a good question." Kate didn't know the answer.

Lacey led him to a mounting block. Taylor stood in front of him and held onto the reins so he couldn't walk forward and Kate held the other stirrup to prevent the saddle from slipping while Lacey climbed on. He stood still like a gentleman. Lacey cued him forward and he listened, eager to please.

The screen door to Miss Della's house clapped shut. She approached the girls with an eager smile on her face, excited to see someone riding her horse.

"You were made to ride him," she said, admiration in her voice. "He acts as if he's been ridden recently."

None of the girls responded. Kate wasn't about to admit the truth.

Lacey walked him around the bare paddock a few times. He stretched his neck long and low, relaxing. The goats in the paddock moved out of their way. He didn't seem to mind the clucking chickens running around, either.

Lacey cued him to trot. Thunder tossed his head a couple of times in argument but then accepted the request. He floated at the trot with

Lacey in perfect rhythm.

Miss Della gasped. "Look at how you ride him! You fit together well."

To Kate's surprise, pride filled her at their accomplishment. If Lacey showed him, not that that was possible, but if she did…she would clean up with blue ribbons. On a selfish note, Kate was glad she didn't have to compete against them. Miss Della was right. They were meant to be together.

When Lacey was finished riding, and after she untacked Thunder, Kate noticed that the other girl was frowning. "What's wrong," Kate asked.

Lacey shook her head, unable to answer.

"Is it because you already miss Thunder?" Kate asked.

Lacey's lower lip stuck out. That was all the answer Kate needed. Without realizing it at first, she touched Lacey's arm. "It's okay. You'll get to see him enough," Kate said.

Lacey frowned but nodded.

"My mom will take us once a week." Kate pulled away from touching Lacey. The contact made her uncomfortable. "I bet your mom would take you once a week too."

"Guess that will have to be enough," Lacey said, returning Thunder to his now cleaned stall. She rubbed his forehead and planted a kiss on his muzzle before she slid the stall door closed. "Who knows when I'll see him again."

CHAPTER THIRTY

The next evening the girls were at the barn. They had ridden their horses and were untacking them in the aisle.

The weather was mild and gorgeous. They had finished riding in a lesson and were chatting with each other, lost in conversation, when Thunder trotted into the barn.

"Thunder!" Lacey jumped up from sitting on the tack trunk.

What was he doing here again? It wasn't storming, so that meant he jumped the fence intentionally.

Razor paced back and forth in the crossties. Thunder approached him to sniff muzzles. Kate, who had just walked away for a moment, picked up her pace to reach her horse before he broke the crossties.

"Come here, boy." Lacey snatched a spare halter off the hook that was fast becoming his.

Thunder wasn't frightened or snorting tonight, so he lowered his head without much encouragement needed and poked his nose into the noseband. "Don't you like Miss Della's?" Lacey asked. He pawed the ground as if making his dislike of the situation known.

"Why does he keep returning to our barn?" Kate asked.

"Horses run back home," Taylor said. "He thinks of this as home."

"But why?" Kate asked. "He has a home with Miss Della."

"Think about it." Taylor unhooked the crossties from her horse Frankie. "If you were a horse, would you prefer Miss Della's lonely farm, or here, where Lacey loves on him like he's her horse?

That was an easy question to answer. Kate understood now.

"I think Layne's still here," Sarah said. She hadn't moved from her favorite position on top of a tack trunk.

"No!" Lacey said. "She'll call Miss Della."

"Exactly the point," Kate said. Why didn't Lacey understand that the horse belonged to someone else.

The sound of clicking heels from cowboy boots on pavement made the girls glance outside the barn. Layne and Miss Della were making their way to them.

"Great," Lacey said under her breath.

The women entered the barn. Thunder raised his head, recognizing Miss Della.

She walked straight to her horse. "Why do you keep running off?" She rubbed her hand along the underside of his jaw. "You like all this attention, don't you?" Thunder tossed his head as if he understood the question.

"I don't blame you." Miss Della turned to face Lacey, who was standing at Thunder's side. "I've been thinking. While I love Thunder, he prefers you. I think he likes the energy and attention he gets from a young rider. I can't ride him anymore. I don't want to sell him, but I'd be open to you riding him."

Lacey didn't say anything. What could she say? She was already riding him.

"Let me make myself clearer," Miss Della said. "Would you want to keep him here."

"You mean as a lease?" Lacey asked. At Miss Della's nod, Lacey said, "I appreciate the offer but my mom can't afford to keep a horse."

"I can understand that," Miss Della said. "They are expensive."

Layne stepped closer. "She's talking about a free lease, Lacey."

Lacey's eyes widened. "Really?" A slow smile lit up her face as Lacey understood what Miss Della and Layne were saying. "You mean he could stay here with me? I can ride him whenever I wanted?"

Miss Della nodded. "We can work out the details, but yes."

Lacey surprised them all by leaping up and down, and then throwing her arms around Miss Della's neck.

When she calmed down, Lacey said, "I need to talk with my mom."

"Why don't I call her tonight," Layne offered. "I'll give her the details. If she hears the plan from me she'll be more likely to realize the great offer Miss Della is extending."

While still holding Thunder's lead rope in her hand, Lacey bounced in front of Layne and wrapped her arms around their trainer. "Thank you! Both of you."

"I'll call your mom tonight," Layne said.

The girls would have to wait until tomorrow at school to find out the answer.

All night long Kate tossed and turned in her bed. Of course she wanted Lacey to lease Thunder. It was in both their best interests. But deep down inside, if Kate truly wanted to be honest with herself, she was fearful that having Thunder at the barn would make Lacey more competitive against her. They were starting to like each other more, but if Thunder was there daily with Lacey leasing him, she would become Kate's biggest competitor. In horse shows they'd have to enter against each other.

Even in lessons, Kate imagined Lacey attempting to outride her.

The thought was more than upsetting.

She tossed and turned. It was midnight, not to mention a school night, and she was still awake. Tomorrow promised to be a long day. Her thoughts revolved around Lacey and Thunder. Guilt pressed down on her for thinking selfishly. Thunder deserved a happy home. He would have one if Lacey leased him. Somehow Kate needed to focus on that fact and not on her own fears. But fears were fears. And the fears refused to leave her.

The next morning, as she knew would happen, Kate dragged out of bed. Her eyes hurt from lack of sleep. Part of her was excited to find out the answer about Thunder, but the other part of her—the anxious part—dreaded knowing.

Despite the exhaustion, Kate dressed quickly, ate her cereal with record speed, and pulled on her backpack by the front door before her mother said a word. When she did, the concern in her voice made Kate more anxious. "Why are you in such a hurry?" her mother asked.

Kate hesitated to think about how much information she wanted to tell her mom. She wasn't ready to admit her true fears, so she decided to stick with the basics. "Thunder returned to the barn last night. He keeps coming back to Lacey, so Miss Della offered to give her a free lease. Layne planned to call Lacey's mom last night, and we find out the answer this morning."

Kate's mom studied Kate. "And from your frown, you don't seem so happy about things."

Her mom tuned in to Kate more than she thought. It was time to be honest, to admit her concerns aloud. "Well, Lacey is competitive. I've had bully issues with her before, and if she leases Thunder, I wonder how that will change barn life."

"That's a real concern," her mother said. She wasn't usually this understanding. Kate couldn't remember the last time they had a thoughtful talk together, where Kate felt her mother was in touch with Kate's complicated emotions.

"I'm proud of you for realizing the possible issues."

Kate didn't know what to say, so she set her heavy backpack on the floor. Her mother took that as a sign to continue the conversation.

"Change isn't all bad. It can be scary because you don't know what to expect, but have faith that it will all work out."

Her mother was right. Kate needed to relax, to take one day at a time. She would deal with the issues as they showed up, not all at once beforehand. "Thanks, mom. I love you." She hugged her mother tight. It had been a long while since Kate had hugged her mother, or for that matter, a long time since she had last said she loved her mom. Mothers needed love too. Kate held on for a long moment. When she pulled back she noticed her mother's eyes were wet from tears.

Kate made a mental note to show affection to her mother more often.

"Let's get you to school," she said, ushering Kate out the door. Was her mother uncomfortable showing her emotions? Probably. That explained why her mom was reserved most of the time.

In addition to the poor night's sleep, all the recent changes left Kate tired. Kate hated change. Interestingly enough, though, a sense of lightness was fast replacing the heavy load she was feeling earlier after she had first woken up. The talk with her mother helped. Kate barely dreaded the news about Thunder. At the very least, if Lacey's mom allowed her to lease Thunder, he would be happy and Lacey would take excellent care of him.

As soon as Kate walked down the hallway at school toward her locker, Lacey bounded toward her. She was beaming with excitement.

"My mom said yes! Thunder is mine!" Lacey snatched Kate into a hug.

Shocked, Kate stood there not knowing what to do. When Lacey didn't let go, Kate wrapped her arms around Lacey too. "Congrats!" Kate was truly happy for the girl. "You and Thunder make a great team."

Lacey let go, did a little hop in place, and

screeched. "He's mine...*mine*. Miss Della kept him overnight at the barn because she was hoping my mom would say yes. Do you want to ride tonight?"

Taylor joined them. "We'd love to ride with you."

"Now I'm officially a part of the jumping club," Lacey said.

Taylor and Kate looked at each other. It still surprised Kate that a bully wanted to join "their" group. Maybe her dad was right. Bullies were people too. And Kate would deal with the competitive side of Lacey one incident at a time.

~~The End~~

ABOUT THE AUTHOR

Lisa Morgan started riding horses when she was in the third grade. She competed on the Hunter Jumper circuit, and eventually became a riding instructor. She has three kids, but only one has inherited her love of horses. Through their experiences, and from many hours spent at the barn, Lisa came up with the Shackleford Banks Series and the Horse Club Series.

She hopes you continue to enjoy her books. Happy reading!

~~Lisa~~

Made in the USA
Columbia, SC
27 April 2020

93719640R00167